Going the Distance

Lee Markowitz

Edited by Jason Ripple

Copyright © Lee Markowitz 2019

All rights reserved. No part of this publication may be reproduced in any form or by any means, including photocopying, recording, or other electronic or mechanical methods, without the prior written permission of the publisher, except in the case of brief quotations embodied in critical reviews and certain other non-commercial uses permitted by copyright law. For permission requests, write to the publisher.

Any person who commits any unauthorized act in relation to this publication may be liable to criminal prosecution and civil claims for damages.

Written permission has been granted by all parties regarding the use of names.

Written December 2017.
First published July 2019.

ISBN 978-0-578-53824-2

Dedications

For Samantha, Alexander, and Matthew...

For Melanie, Adam, Darrin, and Michael...

For Dad...

I love you.

"It ain't about how hard you hit.
It's about how hard you can get hit and keep moving forward.
How much you can take and keep moving forward.

That's how winning is done!"

—Rocky Balboa

Preface

Does anybody have a "normal" childhood? I suppose you or I could surmise a definition for that overused, vague label, but the concept hardly seems realistic, or purposeful. If you stop and think about it for a minute, you could probably jog a few less-than-pleasant memories that prove your parents (or at least one of them) were out of their minds, at times. There were (hopefully) some good times, too. You see, there's a set of variables that comprise childhood and ultimately play a role in shaping who you grow up to be. Things like your zip code, how much money your parent(s) made and how they chose to spend it, how many siblings you had, how you were toilet trained, and other factors we have zero control over, like our parents' health and personal habits. However we categorize childhood—normal, abnormal, or somewhere in the middle—we can't ignore our pasts. We can suppress them if needed, bury disturbing memories deep down and possibly pay the consequences (both psychologically and financially) later on. We can mask pain with humor, shy away from relationships, play the excuse card forever. Or we can face it, deal with it, and move on. Because no matter where we come from, no matter how bad or colorful our pasts might be, as adults, we carry ourselves how we choose.

That has been my focus: the choice. It's a choice we all get to make. It's a choice I had to make.

Even if your childhood was something out of an endearing movie or whimsical storybook, you could likely find something to complain about. But where does complaining get you? It doesn't change anything. It just makes you annoying to those around you. And it's no way to go through life. People who have less-than-perfect childhoods or experience loss or failure or tragedy often choose to use those misfortunes as excuses. That bothers me. A lot. Something bad happened to me, so I'm going to waste what's left of my life, make excuses for things that are my fault, blame anyone I can, and expect pity, sympathy, and hand-outs from anyone and everyone. Yeah, your parents might have screwed you up. Maybe you lost someone close, maybe you lost your job, maybe some bad luck came and kicked you right in the ass. So what? At some point, whether you choose to acknowledge it or not, you can regain control of your life and steer it in the direction you want. You can be lazy or you can work hard. You can be a drain on society and complain your way through life or you can pick your head up and be productive. You can give up or you can stand up.

With that being said, the story that follows is NOT me complaining. It's certainly not me asking for pity. I don't want—or need—sympathy, pats on the back, or to be looked at differently by those who *think* they know all about me already. Having a rough past or dealing with unfortunate tragedies doesn't give you a crutch to lean upon whenever you feel like it, nor does it excuse you from being the best possible version of yourself. We all deal with tragedy. We all face setbacks. And this is, perhaps, how character is born. So no, this is not a book of whining, no need to worry. I am a regular Joe (or Lee) with a somewhat troubling past, and this is my story. Some of it I chose, and some of it chose me. Telling my tale is honestly therapeutic. That might sound selfish, I know. But maybe you'll get something out of it, too. Maybe you can relate to parts. We'll have to wait and see.

If one person reads this and relates to it, if one person takes something tangible from this, if one person's life improves at all because of my openness and honesty (and discomfort resulting from being open and honest), then it's all worth it and I'll consider my goal accomplished.

Most of what follows has never been shared, not even with those closest to me. Some of it has, and my siblings can share at least as much as I can, if not more. Maybe they'll write their own books one day. But I like writing, and I like telling stories, so I chose to write a book. I've never written a book before, but it seemed like a good idea.

Much of what you will read is not pretty, but it is all real. It's all honest. That I promise you.

Oh, and another thing—I don't care much for therapists, or psychoanalysts, or sharing my deepest, darkest thoughts and memories and fears and insecurities with a stranger face-to-face. So, I'll just lay down on the couch and begin by sincerely thanking you for listening (reading).

PART I: Take the Hits

Chapter 1

I remember sitting on the paper-covered table in my pediatrician's office while my mom stood next to me, holding her pocket book tightly and grimacing with frustration. I was used to this routine: the doctor would say a few corny things to try and make me laugh, he'd take the stethoscope from around his shoulders and put the cold piece against my chest, he'd tell me to breathe deeply, I would strain and wheeze loudly like I did the whole night before, I'd cough, he'd say it was bronchitis again, he'd prescribe the usual medicine, remind me to use my breathing machine every four hours, say a few more doctor things, and send me home with my mom.

This time, however, was different. He asked a question he hadn't ever asked before. Looking back, I can only assume (I'm not a doctor) he saw a repetitious pattern and aimed to discover its cause.

"Does anyone smoke in the house?"

I was about to answer, but I was cut off.

"Absolutely not. I never smoke in the house."

Okay, let's pause there for a second. My mom lied to the doctor. No hesitation, no reservation. He was asking an honest question that deserved a forthright answer. I was only a kid, but I was old enough to understand that lying was bad. It wasn't that tough of a concept to get. When he asked, I was going to tell the truth. Why wouldn't I? But my mom lied to him. And even worse, he believed her. My mom smoked all the time. She smoked in the kitchen while she cooked our food. She smoked in the car anytime we went somewhere, including to and from doctors' appointments. She smoked in the den while we watched television. She always had a cigarette in her mouth. And she always had a mean face when she smoked—she would hold the cigarette tightly between her lips so her hands would be free and she would squint slightly as the smoke puffed up into a cloud that rose past her eyes and clung to the walls and the ceiling and our clothes and our lungs and our memories.

It wasn't easy being seven or eight years old and realizing that the things my mom said and did were not right. We grow up, trained and conditioned to take our parents' words and actions as examples to follow. They are our models, after all. And so, it went against my basic instincts to disagree with my mom, to disregard the things she said and did, to realize and try to accept that she was not a good person.

For one thing, she had a terrible mouth. She cursed like a truck driver (no offense to truck drivers). It was a habit she didn't try to prevent us from adopting. I remember being at a friend's house one day during my elementary years. We were playing and having fun, and then his mom threw me out of the house because I used foul language. I cursed at her. I made a comment about the fuckin snacks she had prepared for her son and me. I didn't do it to be mean or disrespectful. I'm not making an excuse—I honestly thought that was a normal, acceptable means of communication. Gave me plenty to think about as I walked home.

    My mother was downright nasty to strangers, too. I remember one time walking through the Costco (it was Price Club then) parking lot with her. We had just finished shopping and had a few items to load into the trunk of her white Mercedes. As we walked through the parking lot, I noticed a mom pushing a baby stroller and pulling a shopping cart piled high with folding chairs. She tried to lift the chairs into the back of her SUV, and it seemed clear that she could have used some help. Her baby was crying loudly. My mom and I were just about at our car, and loading our packages of hotdogs, soda, and cigarettes wouldn't take me too long, so I ran over and offered to help. I was only there for a minute or two; I neatly stacked her chairs while she tended to her baby. She was thankful, and that made me feel good. It wasn't a big deal, but I was happy that I could help her. I knew it was the right thing to do. I got screamed at when I went back to my mom and spent the car ride home getting an earful. "Why would you do that? Why would you go help that bitch when I needed your help? She can lift her own fuckin' chairs. I can't believe how fuckin' selfish you can be."

A half-hour ride home being berated for doing what I thought and knew was right. What do you do with that?

My mother said horribly racist, disgusting things. She verbally trashed our father and all of our paternal relatives to the point where we never saw anyone. Thanksgiving, Hanukkah, birthdays, any holiday or special gathering was to be spent with only our immediate family because everyone else was unworthy, untrustworthy, and/or trashy. Her own mother made the rare trip from Queens and she was, from what I can remember, quite nice. My dad's mom, I remember, was very nice, too. We rarely saw her because, but I enjoyed the visits, especially when she would play old lady card games with me. After she left, my mother would spend days, almost as if she was trying to reprogram us, talking about how horrible of a person our grandmother was, how utterly disgusting and stupid and impolite. It made no sense, but that didn't stop us from having to listen to it.

I remember hearing kids at school talk about how their aunts and uncles and cousins and grandparents would come for holidays, how they would go to grandma's house for some family party, how their cousins were like siblings. I never met my grandfathers because they passed before I was born or shortly thereafter. My dad didn't have too many stories about his dad from what I remember, but my mom filled in the gaps by telling how despicable he was, how uncultured and idiotic. Her dad, according to her descriptions, was the opposite—cultured and refined, hardworking and flawless. I didn't buy it, but I guess it doesn't matter.

I first met my Aunt (dad's side) when I was almost 20. How sad is that? No, she didn't live in a foreign country, but I still had to wait almost twenty years to meet her. I had seen her and her daughter (my first cousin) at my sister's wedding a few years before, but I was not permitted to talk to either besides a quick "hello." My mother had explained, on many occasions, how everyone in my dad's family was garbage. They were bad people with no manners, and we were better off for not seeing them and having them as a part of our lives.

    Well, as it turns out, my cousin is nothing like what my mother had described. And my aunt is an amazing woman. She's as sweet as can be. I've grown to know them both over the past several years, and though I wish I would have had that chance earlier, I'm grateful that they are part of my life now. My aunt, like her daughter, is thoughtful, warm, hospitable, and kind. She hosts holiday dinners sometimes, and when we go to her house, she makes us feel like we're at home. We feel welcome, safe, and loved. It helps that she looks like my dad—the same cheeks and the same warm smile. Over the past few years, I have grown to love my aunt, almost like a mom. I've developed a close relationship with my cousin, too. I try not to think about the wasted years, the decades when my own family was banned from my life and my family's life. It's much healthier to focus on now, on the relationships we have formed, on the closeness we enjoy and cherish.

We were trained to dislike everyone and to trust no one. Anyone who wasn't Jewish was bad. Anyone who was not white was bad. Anyone who didn't have money was trash. Anyone who was Irish or Polish or French was drunk, stupid, and snobby. Anyone related to my father—including my father, of course—was a piece of shit. Don't even get me started on my mother's take on the homosexual population. She, of course, had clever, colorful names for the various demographics that differed from our own. Now, I understand that my parents grew up in a different time, in an era that preceded political correctness and the ever-pressing awareness of others' feelings and everyone being offended by everything, but it seemed extreme nonetheless. I remember thinking about that often. Could everyone in the world be bad? And was that supposed to mean that my mother was good? Didn't add up. Trying to make sense of all this was impossible, particularly when I was a child. Nevertheless, this was how life was in our house.

One of my mother's favorite past times was telling us stories of how bad of a person our father was. My older siblings had cars and friends and jobs and were seldom at home, especially during the summer months. My little brother and I were a forced, trapped audience. Dad would be working, so our mother would corner us at any opportunity and chew our ears off. "Did you know that your father is a criminal? He'll probably end up in jail soon, so don't get used to seeing him around." My father was an entrepreneur, and although I don't know all the ins and outs of the business he had established, I never understood where this assertion came from. It took me years, and I mean years, to conclude that my mother simply hated him and tried desperately to turn us against him. I surmised that her tales of federal agents preparing to pounce during the midnight hours and the cold jail cell that would become his permanent residence were just stories. They were fabrications aimed at turning our heads and hearts against him. It was like a contest she was trying to win. And I remember these stories getting to me. I remember lying in bed at night wondering if the police were going to come and arrest my dad. I remember worrying about being left alone with my mother and not being able to see him anymore. After enough time, I noticed how her stories became more elaborate, more far-fetched, more ridiculous. I finally got to the point where I just let her talk because there was no way to get out of it. Settling on the fact that my father wasn't going anywhere, that there was no truth to what my mother was saying, helped me fall asleep at night. Oh, and for the record, my dad wasn't a criminal and he never went to jail.

Chapter 2

My dad's office was in our basement; however, there was a brief stint where he actually *went* to work. For a few years, he had rented space in a local office building and thought it would be beneficial to conduct his business in a real office. Our mother would take my little brother and me there sometimes during the summer to visit him, but an innocent visit was hardly on my mother's agenda. We'd show up, and they'd argue. They'd scream and curse, usually about money, and my dad's secretary would thoughtfully take my brother and me into the hallway or the coffee lounge or outside for a walk as a reprieve. She knew we didn't need to hear what was going on, and we didn't want to be a part of it. And we grew attached to her for that reason. We felt safe and protected. We didn't have to be afraid of visiting my dad's office because we knew she'd be there. That, of course, did not stop our mother from filling us in on every detail once we got in the car. Then, in the presence of strangers, when she was desperate for attention and pity, she would devour ears, ignore rolling eyes and obnoxiously loud body language of prisoners trying to escape, and say her favorite line, "Unfortunately, the kids know everything that's going on." *Unfortunately.* How is it unfortunate when you deliberately tell us everything?

There is no excuse to do that to your kids. Yes, kids have to grow up, and sure, there is something to be said for being open and honest with your children, but kids have a right to their inherent, God-given innocence. A three-year-old should worry about squeezing in another episode of a favorite cartoon before bed. An eight-year-old should be concerned about what kind of snacks are in the pantry. A young teenager should be focusing on school and sports and friends and acne. So no, your kids don't have to know about every dirty detail of your life, even if they are your only audience. "I like to be honest with them" functions as a lovely but shitty excuse.

Anyway, I guess we all knew what was going to happen. We all saw it coming. On

Saturday mornings, my dad would take my little brother and me to the park to play baseball—one of my favorite childhood memories. We would pack our gloves and bats and balls into his trunk, play for hours under the summer sun, and then hit the local deli for lunch before returning home. My dad's secretary showed up a few times with her daughters, and we all enjoyed playing together while the two of them stood by and talked. *Our* mother's talks had shifted gears. Instead of the dad-is-going-to-jail bit or the I'm-the-better-parent tale, we got the your-piece-of-shit-father-is-no-doubt-fucking-his-secretary treatise. Not to risk salvaging any degree of youthful, blissful ignorance, we were privy to the juicy details of what she imagined the two were doing together. "She probably sucks his dick before he fucks her. I bet he fucks her right in the office, right on his fucking desk." She became enraged when we would speak of her (we still liked her regardless of what she and our dad were/were not doing), so we were required to refer to her as "whore." I wish I were making this up. And if you are reading this thinking I have paraphrased language or added f-bombs for effect, you are mistaken. We—my little brother and me, who were about five and ten years old, respectively—referred to our dad's secretary as "whore," regardless of the setting. The supermarket, the dinner table, at school, it didn't matter. If we failed to do so at any point, we were reprimanded and reminded of the set expectations. I remember how upset and frustrated my dad appeared every time we said it, so we tried to avoid bringing her up in conversation. It was only when our mother ignited the topic, which was quite often, that we had to play along.

As it turns out, my father did have an affair with this woman.

I am not excusing it, nor am I justifying it, but I do find it interesting how our ideals and moral compasses shift as we age, through experience. As a child, I could never understand how a man and a woman could exchange marital vows, promise to be honest and loyal to one another, and then cheat. As an adult, I can better understand (I still don't condone or excuse it) why and how these things happen, but pre-pubescent me had a tough time digesting it. The ironic thing is that I never really held it against him. I knew (it was more than obvious) that there was no love in my parents' marriage. I knew they hated each other, and I witnessed how they treated each other. My father, I suppose, found someone he felt comfortable with, someone he trusted, someone he wanted. They cared about each other, and they enjoyed being together. And when it came out that afternoon in our house and my mother's screams could be heard for miles as my brother and I hid upstairs, I felt oddly relieved. My mother had drummed it up for months, and it was only a matter of time.

The days and weeks after that got really bad. My mother would spend her days screaming profanities and asking graphic sexual questions in front of us, purposely in front of us. We'd be sitting in the den watching television, and she'd start in with questions of how and for how long and where. My dad wouldn't engage, but rather sat silently, knowing no response would suffice. She went into my dad's closet one day while he was working and took all of his clothes and bagged them up and brought them to the dumpster. She made my brother and I go along to help. She used the car ride to explain the various sexual positions my father and his mistress had likely engaged in, what it meant to give a "real" blowjob, the ways my father was unsatisfactory in the bedroom, and how anytime our father wasn't at home meant he "was getting his cock sucked and fucked." Then we threw his clothes out, all of them, because "that's what he wore when they fucked."

Now, I can understand a woman feeling devastated by her husband's infidelity, so I get her acting out. I just wish my brother and I didn't have to be indulged with all the wonderful details and creative imagery. Learning what a blowjob is in this context was not my idea of a birds and bees chat. *Unfortunately, the children know everything.* Unfortunately, my ass.

Chapter 3

I didn't understand her. Never could. Never will. Moms are supposed to be caring and thoughtful and sweet and loving and protective and honest. They're supposed to bake cookies and brownies and give hugs and tell neat stories and make sure you brush your teeth and tell you to clean your room and love you. They're supposed to love you. They're supposed to tell you to come inside when it rains and make sure your homework gets done. They are supposed to enforce curfews, they are supposed to encourage you to do your best, raise you to be kind. They are supposed to kiss your cheeks, kiss your boo-boos, be proud of you, and make sure you are healthy. They are supposed to love you. My mother was—and still is—the worst person I have ever known. I'm sure that sounds horrible, and I wish I was saying it for effect. But it's true. I have never met a more horrible person in my life.

Another thing that upsets me to no end is the fact that I have, unavoidably, adopted some traits from her, attributes I can't ignore. But I suppose we are all a mixture of our upbringings, and with the good comes the fugly.

Thinking again about that doctor's appointment, I remember we left the office that morning, got into her car and drove toward the pharmacy. We weren't out of the doctor's parking lot before my mom lit up a cigarette. And she was too cold to open the window, even the back one. So I sat behind her in her white Mercedes, trying to get a full breath of any kind of air I could get. She screamed at me because I made her take me to the doctor. I didn't *make her* take me. I had been up the whole night before, coughing and wheezing, trying to breathe. But she had things to do, and my bronchitis was an untimely, inconvenient pain in her ass. This was a routine I had grown used to, much like drowning her out with my own thoughts. So I sat there, breathing in the smoke and thinking about baseball to pass the time. I hated the way the cigarette smoke smelled. It's suffocating. Truthfully, it still gives me a headache to this day.

By the time I was about ten or twelve, my pediatrician prescribed me an inhaler that I could keep with me. I liked the inhaler much better than the breathing machine we had set up on our kitchen counter because of its portability and efficiency. It eventually got me out of what was an inescapable before-bedtime ritual: I'd stand by the counter and watch my mom crack open the little vial of medicine and pour it into the plastic cup and attach the tube that connected to the mouth piece. She held the cigarette in her mouth, her whole face drawn around it. Then she'd hand me the green plastic thing that I put over my mouth and nose, and I'd put the strap around my head, and I'd breathe as deeply as I could for the next five minutes. I remember my pediatrician explaining that it was important to take deep breaths so the medicine could do its job. My mom stood facing me, smoking her cigarette, and yelling about how expensive my fuckin medicine was. She had to yell louder than usual because the breathing machine was noisy. I took deep breaths. I remember staring at the digital clock on our oven and waiting for the minute to change so I could start my rhythmic count to sixty over again, like a coping mechanism. After five minutes, the breathing machine would start to putter and the mist that came from it wouldn't go so high. That meant it was done and I could go in the den with my dad for a little while before bed.

Chapter 4

I don't remember what my bedtime was—or even if I had a specified bedtime—but I do remember that I finished the breathing machine by around the third or fourth inning of the Mets game. (Enough about mother for a minute; I need a break.) My dad had his spot on the couch that sat against the wall under the window. Even though the couch faced the middle of the den, we never sat that way. Dad would sit on one side so he could face the television that was in the corner, and when I came in, he'd move his feet so I could sit at other end. I can close my eyes and still see that old, worn-out couch and our 32" Zenith television and that big, three-pane window that looked out to our front yard. And I can still see my dad sitting there, smiling every time the Mets got a hit and using the breaks between pitches to teach me about the game he loved so much. Spending evenings with him watching Mets games was the best part of my day and still one of my fondest, most vivid memories of childhood.

I was born in 1981, and the New York Mets won the World Series in '86. I wish I could say I remember it, but all I truthfully recall about that series comes from stories I have heard and the video replays of the infamous ball through Buckner's legs—I've seen it a thousand times. My dad was a big Mets fan, and he started teaching me about baseball when I was little. I suppose any kid could relate to this—maybe it's part of the dad-son handbook or something. Maybe it's something that naturally connects fathers to their sons. My older brother used to talk to my dad about cars. That was their thing. But for me, for us, it was baseball.

He began with the basics: 3 strikes or 4 balls, the difference between foul and fair, the infield positions, the outfield positions, the numbers of the positions so you could understand when the announcer called a 6-4-3 double play, pinch hitters, and why the American League wasn't as good because the pitchers didn't hit (those teams didn't have to strategize the way the National League teams did.) As time went on, we graduated to discussions of more complex terms and tactics: the suicide squeeze, the double steal, the hit-and-run that should have been used more often, when to pull the pitcher (this was, thankfully, before the age of the almighty pitch count) and when and how to lay a bunt. I watched the Mets game with him every night. He taught me about the history of the game, about how upset he was when the Dodgers moved out of Brooklyn, about the year they beat the Goddamn Yankees (sorry, Samantha) and how the Mets got their colors—the blue from the Brooklyn Dodgers and the orange from the New York Giants. He (and every other Dodgers fan, as I was told) was crestfallen when they uprooted and headed to California, and becoming a Yankees fan was downright laughable. So there we were—devout Mets fans and annual repeaters of "There's always next year."

No, my childhood was not perfect. And no, my mother didn't qualify for any parent-of-the-year awards. And you know what? My father wasn't perfect either. No parents are. Sure, some are better than others, but nobody is perfect. (Sorry for the cliché, but it's true.) He had his flaws, he made his mistakes, and I'm sure he could bang out a list of regrets. But I didn't need a perfect father. I needed my dad. He loved me. He loved all of his kids, all five of us. He showed us that he loved us. He showed that you don't have to be perfect to be a good parent. You just have to love your kids.

Those evenings watching baseball with my dad weren't fancy or extravagant. It was simple, and it was real. It was time we spent together, a loving father and his adoring son, and it was awesome. I love baseball, I love the Mets, and I love my dad.

Chapter 5

I was almost five years old when my little brother was born in the spring of 1986. At that time, my dad worked in the basement. We had a relatively expansive house in Port Jefferson and the basement had a spare bedroom, a small tiled bathroom, an unfinished but spacious laundry room, and my dad's office. For as long as I can remember, my dad slept in that spare bedroom. He woke up sometime between five and six, took a shower, shaved, got dressed, and went to work. He filled his coffee pot and steadily drank it until his break around noon when he'd go to the local bank and the post office. During the summer months, I'd go with him to run his errands. It was a short trip, but it was a welcomed routine and it got me out of the house. He'd let me hand the banking papers to the teller, and I'd act surprised when she gave me a lollipop. Then we'd return home, he'd go back to work and I would do whatever I could to avoid my mother. He came upstairs a few minutes after five o'clock every day, just in time for dinner.

As a kid, I couldn't understand why my dad slept in the basement instead of with my mother. Why didn't they sleep in the same bed? Isn't that what parents are supposed to do? I figured it out as I got older. It was the only way they could coexist. The only way they could make it work. Their marriage was as devoid of love as it was normalcy. Ironically, as miserable as they were and with as much ferocity as they hated one another, the word "divorce" was seldom spoken, although it was thrown around sporadically during especially heated battles. They stayed together, perhaps, because they thought it would be the best thing for the kids. That's a heaping load of irony right there. Granted, I had no control over this. Neither did my three brothers or my sister. We were pawns. And I'm well aware—as we all are—of the potential damage that divorce has on kids. It's not an ideal situation for any parties concerned. But I'll tell ya', I would have gladly taken those odds as a kid who was terrified of his own house.

I hear married people say that often enough. The notion that staying together is what's best for the kids. But living in a house where a mom and a dad despise each other, where the hatred and the tension are palpable is not the "best thing for the kids."

I remember thinking about my parents getting a divorce. It had a clear upside: end this shitshow, say "bye-bye" to mommy dearest, and salvage what was left of a childhood. But I also remember considering the other perspective. I remember thinking about the possibility of ending up with my mother. That would have been even more torturous—the thought of living with my mother without having the balance that my dad provided as best he could makes me cringe. Had I the chance to live with my father, that would have been a different story, and this would be a different story. But it's nothing I can change now. I guess everything happens for a reason. (I hear people say that a lot.) My parents didn't get a divorce. They stayed together. They hated each other, they slept in different beds, in different rooms, on different floors, and they spent the decades of their marriage fighting and arguing. It is what it is, as they say.

I thought of running away. Actually, I thought of it rather often. What kid doesn't, right? I remember staying up at night calculating how far I could get, where I could sleep, what I would eat. Unfortunately, a seven- or eight- or ten- or fourteen-year-old doesn't have many resources, like a car or money or a clue, and reality always slapped me in the face. I couldn't run away. I couldn't escape. This was my house, my life. I was trapped.

Chapter 6

More often than not, my dad would go back downstairs after dinner and keep working until the Mets game started shortly after seven. He worked on Saturday mornings while we slept in. He saved Saturday afternoons and Sundays for yard work and fixing stuff around the house; for taking my little brother and me to play baseball at the park, or for taking my older brother along, too, to go to the local car dealers to sit in the new cars and play with the buttons. Granted, my dad worked a lot, but he always made time for us, and we never felt slighted because of his stringent schedule. We didn't take many family vacations, but that might be a blessing that needs no disguise. Weekends at the park and weeknights with the Mets worked just fine.

Summers were interesting. You know the last few days in June when kids sit in their classrooms and peer yearningly out the windows at the grass and the sunlight and the warmth and the endless possibilities that summer promises? They daydream about being home, sleeping in, going to the beach, drinking in a season of freedom and fun, and not being stuck inside of hot classrooms with annoying teachers. Everyone looked forward to that final bell, that moment when entrapment ended and the glorious euphoria of summer began. I could see it in their faces. The excitement, the anticipation.

    Those weren't exactly my thoughts. Don't get me wrong, I hated school. I had virtually no friends until high school because I cursed like my mother and discovered the hard way that people—like other kids' parents—don't like that. The first time I hung out with a friend was usually the last time, and it took me a little while to do the math. Plus, I battled (That might be the wrong verb—'battled' suggests a winnable fight, and it never felt like I had a chance.) a weight problem for a large portion of my childhood until around my junior/senior year of high school. I was socially awkward, never felt comfortable around other people, never wore trendy clothing or sported an "in" haircut. I had new clothes, but never looked good in them. My mother took advantage of sales by doing the winter shopping at the end of summer when the selection was crappy and the styles were crappier. And we all know how nice and understanding kids are when other kids don't follow popular trends.

    Once, I needed a new folder for one of my classes. It was during elementary school, when kids can be particularly cruel. A simple, two-pocket folder was what the teacher ordered. I scanned the room to check out what other kids had. Some had sports teams; others had various movie characters or athletes. A few had plain, solid-color ones. That was my ticket, a plain blue one. Can't go wrong there. No risk of getting the wrong team or something like that. So I went home and asked my mom. I spelled it out for her. "Please, no characters, no designs, just a plain two-pocket folder." After yelling at me for having to go spend money, she reluctantly snatched her pocketbook from the counter and took off. She returned a half-hour later with my new folder in a plastic bag. As soon as I saw it, I knew life was over. I kept it in my bag, and when nobody in the class was looking, I took it out, slid it into my desk, and hid it under some notebooks and snacks. Had to come out eventually though, right? And that's when I heard it. I heard it loud, and I heard it from everyone. I didn't even know who the "New Kids on the Block" were, but I surmised, quite quickly, that they were not popular. Yeah, a solid-color folder would have been nice. That torment did not end quickly; it seemed to last the whole year, and every time the teacher asked us to take out our folder, I cringed. Now I know that's not a major thing, but for a short, fat kid who wore thick glasses and had no friends, it was a big deal. I wouldn't think of asking for a new one, so I sucked it up and moved forward.

So yeah, school all around sucked for me. Girls had zero interest in me because I wasn't popular and wasn't allowed to play sports like the cool kids. And the cool kids rejected me because I had nothing to contribute to their conversations about last night's game or yesterday's practice or that cool party that everyone enjoyed. I hated going to school. But I knew what awaited me in the summer, and I'd take school over that without a hesitation. School was, at the very least, safe. Sure, my teachers would yell at me for not doing my homework or scold me for doing poorly on a test or something like that, and yes, I was made fun of for being fat and having stupid folders and wearing lame clothes, but nobody hit me. Nobody even threatened to hit me. Nobody, with the exception of my sixth grade English teacher, aimed to deliberately embarrass or belittle me on a level deeper than clothing and fatness and school supplies. Nobody knew me well enough to dig deeper. My sixth grade English teacher was a witch and a half, but that's a story I'd rather not get into. Regardless, while my classmates were counting down the final June seconds, I was dreading summer's hot breath.

      When summer finally came, I worked a routine as best I could. I would sleep in as long as possible until my mother screamed her way into my room and forced me to get up because sleeping past nine AM "wasn't necessary." I wasn't really sleeping though. I'd actually wake up earlier but pretend to sleep so I could be left alone. Less awake time meant less time being forced to listen to her carefully crafted stories. Then it was breakfast time: some sugary cereal in a bowl with milk and a glass of orange juice that my mother insisted on heating up in the microwave that I had to finish. I told her I didn't like it, but she did it anyway. I would sit in my blue chair at the large, rectangular Formica kitchen table, and try my best to eat quickly and not make a mess.

    One early-summer morning, I accidentally spilled some of the milk from the cereal bowl onto the table. I don't know how I did it, and I certainly didn't mean to spill it. I think it was because I was trying to devour my meal as quickly as possible. Anyway, none got on the floor; the mess was contained on the surface of the table in a tiny harmless puddle next to my bowl, and I could have quickly wiped it up with a napkin or two. And to this day, I feel anxious when I see a mess. Even a drop of milk on a counter throws me. I race to clean it. I can't even sit and finish my dinner without getting up to start the dishes. As soon as I finish inhaling my food (a habit I seem incapable of breaking), I'm rinsing the plate and silverware in the sink, I'm loading the dishwasher, I'm spraying and wiping the counters, and I'm driving Samantha absolutely crazy. But I can't help myself. It doesn't make logical sense. I should just sit and enjoy my meal and take my time and then worry about cleaning up. It's a compulsion, and one I cannot control.

Anyway, there I was, about to grab a napkin and wipe up the milk. I didn't get the chance. My mother habitually stood over me or sat too close while I ate and used my being forced to sit as a chance to go off about how horrible my father was and how much she hated him and all the reasons why, all while she puffed away on her successive cigarettes. That, and she'd scream at me to hurry up and finish my goddamn meal (not that I wanted to prolong the experience). My spilled milk interrupted her, and she got angry. She yelled and cursed and slapped me across the face, and then dragged me into the basement laundry room, closed the door, and made me stay there. I don't remember how long I stood there, but I do remember it was dark, it smelled musty and dusty and I had trouble breathing after a while; and I was still hungry. I was in there long enough to miss lunch, too. I didn't mean to spill the milk, and I was meticulously careful never to do it again.

    Summer had begun.

Chapter 7

I remember a sunny summer weekday afternoon. I must have been about five or six, because my little brother was napping in his crib in our den. That's where the television was and where all my toys were. The den was right above my dad's office, and this was one day when my mother was downstairs working in the office with my dad. Occasionally, she "worked" downstairs doing computer stuff or yelling at him for some reason or another or complaining about money and then proclaiming how he couldn't get by without her help. This was one of those days. My older brother and I were playing, and there were cartoons on. I'll admit we were being rambunctious. My little brother woke up from his nap and started crying. Loudly.

When we heard footsteps racing up the basement stairs, my older brother ran out of the den and flew upstairs. I can't say I blame him; I'm just jealous I didn't think and react that quickly. His life experience had taught him a virtual certainty: don't be in that room when she comes in because whatever happens will not be good. I wasn't that seasoned, so I stood by the crib, looking over the top at my brother who was laying on his back and crying. I didn't know what else to do. My mother burst into the den and started screaming at me. I thought she was going to pick him up or do something about his crying, but she was focused on me for some reason. Although I don't remember exactly what she said, I do remember her wrapping her hands around my throat and squeezing tightly. I couldn't breathe. I couldn't swallow. I couldn't move. I don't know why, but I started to pee. I panicked. I remember feeling the warm liquid run down my leg, and I remember hoping it wouldn't get on the carpet. I was trying to stop the pee and trying to breathe, hoping I could wait it out, hoping she would just let go and go back downstairs. No such luck. She looked down and noticed that my pants were wet, so she let go of my throat and grabbed me by my shirt and pulled me down the stairs into the basement and into the small bathroom that was just across from the stairs. She yanked my pants down and told me to stand there in front of the toilet until I was done being a baby. She screamed a few more things at me before she smacked me on my ass and finally left me alone. I remember just standing there. I didn't have to pee anymore since I just went, but I didn't know how long I was supposed to stay. I didn't dare move. After a couple hours, she came back into the bathroom and turned off the light and closed the door. Then she left again. I remember how pitch black it was in there. No windows, not even light from under the door. Even if I wanted or had to pee, I couldn't see what I was doing. And accidentally peeing on the floor or the seat wasn't worth the risk. I stood there for a long time. I didn't pee. And I didn't mean to wake up my little brother, either.

  Eventually she came back. I didn't know what else she was going to do, but having light instead of dark was a plus. She told me to pull up my pants and follow her upstairs. When I walked into the den, she made me pull my pants down again and lay on the floor. She put one of my little brother's diapers on me and made me wear it for the rest of the day. She said this is what happens when you're a baby and you piss in your pants. I remember it was tight and my pants felt funny around it. And I didn't know if I was supposed to pee in them or not, so I just held in whatever I had to do. I think she forgot about it because I took it off before I went to sleep. I was afraid to go into that bathroom for a long time after that, and from that day on, I brought my toys into the kitchen and played there so my little brother could nap and so she couldn't hear me from the basement office. I learned from experience, too.

Chapter 8

We rarely took vacations because my dad worked a lot. That's not a complaint; it's an understandable fact. He owned his own business, worked out of the basement, and if he wasn't there to do the work, the work didn't get done and the bills didn't get paid. That's how he explained it. Made sense.

But occasionally, we'd take a weekend road trip somewhere not too far. It was always a road trip because my mother didn't trust airlines. Or pilots or baggage handlers or runway directors or anyone in the airport. If asked, I'm sure she'd have something to say about the guy mopping the bathroom floor or the lady ringing up gum and magazines in the gift shop. So yeah, road trips.

No complaints, though. I love road trips. Still do. Got snacks, got the license plate game (the era before smart phones and flat screens and social media and kids' faces being glued to screens), got my brothers with whom I'd share the back seat and piss off both parents. Nothing but time and anticipation and an earful of my mother's thoughts and rantings.

    We took a trip to an amusement park one weekend. It was a relatively big one, not too far away. I don't remember the name of it, but it had two sections: a water park and a park with roller coasters and other rides. The plan was to spend a day at each. It took a few hours or so to get there, and my mother was exceptionally irritable the whole time. She was mad before we even got in the car. She didn't approve of our going to an amusement park because it lacked educational value, cultural exposure (because she was so open-minded to other cultures), or any legitimate purpose. It was just a place to, well, be amused. My dad knew we liked amusement parks and tried his best to make summer trips fun so they wouldn't feel like school. My two brothers and I sat in the back seat and listened to our mother call our father an uneducated piece of shit and berate him for his inept parenting. She was pissed at us, too. I don't know why, but why not?

When we got to the water park and changed into our bathing suits, we put our clothes into these small lockers that came with keys that go around your wrist so you don't lose them. My mother insisted on holding all of the keys because we couldn't be trusted with them. Come to think of it, we never even had keys to our own house because "we'd be fuckin' morons and lose them" even though I don't remember losing anything. We had to ring the doorbell and be let in if we were out somewhere. I always thought that was odd.

    Sorry, back to the water park. It was a hot, sunny day. One of those days where the humidity is oppressive and the sun is free from any cloud coverage. My mother decided to sit near the snack area and not be a part of going on rides or smiling, which was just fine by the rest of us. She could stay there all day if she wanted to while we had fun with dad going on the water slides and enjoying the day. Around lunch time, we went back to where she was and found her smoking a cigarette and looking angry. Her eyes got big when she saw me.

Apparently, my shoulders got too much sun, and I was on my way to a sunburn. We didn't bother with sunscreen, so whatever sun hit you, you dealt with. My dad took my brothers to stand on the never-ending line at the snack stand to get food and left me with my mother. I remember each table had its own giant umbrella which stretched far enough to give shade to everyone seated at the table, including my mother. I was about to sit down, but was told not to. She said that because I wanted to come to an amusement park so badly, I could deal with the fuckin' sunburn. So she made me pull my chair out from under the cover of the umbrella and sit so my shoulders were directly in the sun. It didn't take too long for it to hurt, and I could feel my back and shoulders and neck getting redder and hotter. She kept yelling and cursing while other families watched and listened. Some even pointed. And thinking about the sunburn while the sun was beating on me made it worse. I wasn't even hungry anymore. Some cream or ointment would have helped if I were allowed any when I got home, but you can guess how that went. I remember feeling everyone's eyes. There were looking at me and listening to her, and I can only wonder what they were thinking.

Every now and then, I try to objectively examine one of these memories to see if I can give her some benefit of the doubt. Perhaps some explanation or justification. All I can think of is that she must have suffered from some kind of mental illness. Come to think of it, she did mention a therapist at one point. I remember sitting in the kitchen with her, listening to another episode of the nutjob mother show, and being taken aback by this one particular story. She explained how she and my father had seen a therapist years before, early in their marriage. She didn't divulge the reason for their visit, but she said they spoke as a couple and then as individuals before having a consultation at the end. She told me that the therapist realized quickly that my mother was a rational thinker, a pragmatist, and my father was impulsive, incapable of handling challenging situations, short-tempered, and in need of regular therapy. She also said that my dad became so enraged by the therapist's findings that he refused to return for treatment.

    None of that added up. In fact, it seemed like she pulled a switch there, because everything did make sense if you swapped patients. Maybe this story fell into the all-too-familiar category of her trying to make herself seem the better parent. Maybe if she just listened, maybe if she allowed herself to get help, all our lives would have been different. So perhaps there was a mental illness that could have been helped had she continued therapy way back when, but that ship has long since sailed. So no, I can't justify her ways. I can't make sense of the things she said and did, how she treated us, how she proclaims to have raised five children when all any of us remember from her parenting is one horrible nightmare after another, or what in the hell my father ever saw in her. I can't understand it, but maybe it's not for me to understand. It's part of who I am, I won't deny that. But it's a part of me I'm not proud of. If I remain objective in my own self-assessment, I do have a number of not-so-wonderful qualities. Who doesn't? And, as anyone could, I can attribute them to my upbringing. I am impulsive, sometimes my temper isn't as long-fused as I'd like, I hate messes, I become anxious easily, I don't like the summer weather or the sun, I'm a compulsive nail-biter (although I really am working on this one), and I often long for solitude because of the non-threatening peace and quiet. I am, in many regards, an introvert.

    But that's not all I am. Yes, I have these and other qualities I'm not proud of, yes, I see my mother in some things I do (which drives me crazy), but I choose not to let these attributes define me. I have good qualities, too. I promise. They came from my dad. And I'm proud of them. I'm proud that I don't let my past dictate the kind of person I am, that I don't let my negative qualities outweigh my positive ones. I'm proud that I look like my dad, that I have his sarcastic, witty sense of humor, that I have his love for children, and that I'm a devoted Mets fan. I'm proud that I look at things rationally, like he did and that I have an easy smile. I'm proud to be his son.

Chapter 9

My mother loved the sun. She was quite a fan of sunbathing, especially during the long, hot summer days while my dad was downstairs working. My brothers and I kept to ourselves as much as possible, and we looked forward to especially sunny days because that sometimes meant mother would spend a chunk of daylight outside and would leave us the hell alone. Up until around middle school, thankfully, she kept the bottom part of her bathing suits on. Not the top. I knew what a "pair of tits" looked like well before any of my friends got their hands on a porno magazine (before smart phones, remember) or made imaginative sense between the blue and white squiggles on the channels their parents didn't pay for.

Once middle school hit, for whatever reason, she no longer felt it necessary to conceal her bottom half, so she'd lay on her tri-fold beach chair on our deck, completely naked, and bask in the rays for hours.

One day in the early fall of my senior year of high school when the weather was still summer-like, a friend came over without telling me first. Usually, if given advanced notice, I could intercept a visitor outside by the garage doors and save having to explain why my mother was nude for all the world to see. But not this time. He was picking me up to go somewhere, and I truly wished he would have given me warning. He wishes so, too.

He showed up, was let in by my dad (who I can only suppose had become numb to the nudist colony that was our main floor), and walked upstairs—past the French doors that led out onto our deck, which you had to pass to get upstairs to where my room was. He got an eyeful of everything that most women tactfully and relentlessly try to cover. Yep, there was my mother—laying on her back, fully nude, legs spread to ensure an even tan in the afternoon sun.

Speaking honestly, that friend and I still laugh about it to this day.

He and I were quite close in the latter years of high school, and we've thankfully remained friends since. He'll forever be one of my best friends, and I still feel bad for him and what he saw that fateful afternoon. Nobody should have to see that.

Chapter 10

My older brother and I were in the kitchen one summer afternoon, and he took a piece of candy out of the drawer in the refrigerator. We had a wide drawer in the center of our fridge that was filled to the max and perpetually replenished with candy. From a kid's perspective, this was amazing. My parents didn't concern themselves with nutrition (possibly a result of the time in which nutrition didn't concern many), so it was open season on any and all snacks, cookies, candy, etc. The scavenged pastries and Entenmann's boxes on the counter were replaced weekly. Soda, our predominantly consumed beverage, was found in two-liter bottles and steadily depleted as the week progressed. Needless to say, my siblings and I have dealt with perpetual weight issues. To this day, I have to work diligently to keep my weight and belly fat in check. It's honestly disgusting the way we ate. No rules. No limits. No dietary restrictions, no consideration of caloric or fat or sugar intake. No ratios or protein requirements, no limits on bread or pasta consumption, and no education to be had about the importance of healthy eating habits. Forced empty plates and desserts available at any time. I can't remember ever seeing glasses of water or bowls of fruit on the kitchen table. It was either soda or soda to drink. And only whole milk, of course, for breakfast cereal. No food pyramid had any place in our kitchen.

On this particular afternoon, as my older brother and I convened in the kitchen for a habitual mid-morning snacking feast, he unwrapped a piece of candy, put it in his mouth, and chewed it for a few seconds. Then he spit it into the trash. I guess he didn't like it. Then he walked upstairs. I didn't think anything of it. I just stayed in the kitchen, playing with my toys on the floor while popping fun-sized snickers like they were Tic-Tacs. My mother walked into the kitchen a few minutes later and coincidentally had to throw something out. She opened the lid and peered into the trash. She asked me what was in the garbage, so I told her. I only assumed she was referring to my older brother's recently discarded candy. She asked me again. I didn't understand why she repeated her question, but I repeated my answer. I didn't understand her next question. She asked me if I threw-up in the garbage. I thought it was a silly question, because it was only a piece of candy, and throw-up would make a much bigger mess and it would have that nasty throw-up smell. Plus, throw-up goes in the toilet. Feeling puzzled, but oddly threatened at the same time (learning from experience, right), I repeated my answer. She smacked me in the mouth with her open hand and told me that's what happens when you lie. My lips started to bleed from being smashed against my front teeth, and I cried. I ran upstairs to the bathroom and sat on the toilet while blood ran out of my mouth and over my hands and down the front of my shirt. I could still hear her screaming at me from downstairs, about how I was "a fuckin liar who couldn't be trusted" and how disgusting I was for having thrown up in the garbage can.

  My sister came in and asked what happened. She left and came back a minute later with some ice wrapped in a towel. She wiped the blood off my face and told me to put the ice over my mouth before washing my hands in the sink. She sat with me for a while until my bleeding and crying subsided. I didn't lie though. I told the truth. I told the truth and got smacked in the mouth. Lesson learned.

Adults will tell you that lying is often necessary (ever seen *Liar Liar*?). You lie to get out of things, you lie to make people feel better, you lie because it's a vital component of regular communication. We don't tell our bosses how we really feel about having to work late or the effectiveness (or ineffectiveness) of their leadership, we don't reveal to children the truth behind their Christmas presents and lost teeth funds, and we really don't even think twice when we creatively fabricate our way through the day. My mother lied consistently and creatively. And I figured out, at an early age, when she was lying and how habitual it was for her. Maybe she even believed what she was saying, I don't know. There is a diagnosis for that, I think. I knew she was lying when she told me stories about my father's criminalistics tendencies and subpar childhood that wasn't as refined as her own. I knew she was lying when she happily recalled and shared with strangers the cherished moments from my siblings' enamored childhoods, tales that craftily painted her as the quintessential mother figure. That always angered me. I knew she was lying when she pretended to give a shit about our well-being. She didn't play that one off too well.

Lying is an understandably ironic reality, but one an adult can grasp. A kid, not so much. That forced me to grow up a bit faster than I would have liked. I realized that I had to lie, that I had to give short, terse responses, that I had to foresee possible repercussions, and that I had to carefully navigate conversations, which essentially contradicts the often-adored innocent, unfiltered speech that we expect from children. Nothing I can do about it now—just a life lesson learned.

Chapter 11

We all assume traits from our parents, some more desirable than others. It's not something we can control. It's something we occasionally prefer not to acknowledge, but it's there. I fight with Samantha often (not really 'fight'—more like I incessantly annoy her) because I am a complete neat freak. Everything has to have its place, nothing can be on any counters, nothing needs to be saved, everything that could possibly be considered expendable must be expeditiously discarded—and don't even get me started on organization. If there is a mess on the floor or miscellaneous items cluttering a counter in the kitchen, I instantly feel the press of anxiety. I don't think the OCD label does me justice. Did I get this from my mother? Probably. And I'm sorry. I don't want to be like this, and I'm honestly envious of those who don't stress obsessively over the little things like I do. As sick as it sounds, I actually get therapeutic pleasure from taking out the garbage, as if I'm ridding the house of clutter or vermin or disease. I fill up a giant garbage bag—you know, the big, black ones used for fall cleanups—and I feel a genuine sense of relief and accomplishment and satisfaction when I place it at the curb and watch it get taken away.

Parents often tell their kids to clean their rooms. It's a common practice, I think. It's in the first chapter of the parenthood handbook. Sometimes parents yell when their kids don't do it. Sometimes they even threaten to throw things out or take things away. I understand parental frustration and wanting to keep your house neat, and I agree that kids should learn about responsibility and the importance of cleanliness, organization, and complying with what their parents ask. In addition, there is a valuable lesson to be learned: the need to show respect to the people who own the house and provide for you by doing your part and keeping your space within that realm tidy. It shows respect.

My mother took this to the extreme, one could say. It was never predictable, like when a drill sergeant conducts random room inspections, so you have to keep your sleeping quarters impeccable at all times. It happened every couple of months at random, with no warning; there was no way to prepare. My mother would get a bug up her ass, thinking that my room wasn't clean enough, or that I had too many personal belongings, like stories I'd write or seemingly meaningless yet oddly sentimental keepsakes, like old tickets to Mets games. No room for any of that.

  She'd storm into my room with two or three of those big, black garbage bags. She'd systematically go drawer by drawer, throwing out anything she deemed "not necessary" while I sat on my bed and watched in silence. She'd scream throughout the process about how much of a fuckin' moron I was for keeping stupid shit, how I likely got that habit from my asshole father, how I made a mess of her house, and how much of a burden my siblings and I were. The bag would quickly fill as the drawers emptied, and then she'd move onto the closet, under the bed, any spot in which I might attempt to hide or preserve something that I deemed worthy of hanging onto. If the bag got too full, it was my job to take it downstairs and throw my own belongings in garbage, and return with an empty bag so the process could continue. When she had exhausted herself and felt the task was complete, she'd walk out and leave me there. I remember sitting on my bed, trying to process what just happened. It felt like a tornado had just torn through my room. I'd try to cope with what was discarded. It didn't take too long for me to reevaluate the purpose of personal possessions and wonder if it was worth keeping anything. Worst of all, I remember being plagued by an awful irony—I always kept my room clean.

Chapter 12

This one hurt.

My dad came into my room one summer morning. It was early in the summer, just a week or so after the school year had ended. We were quite young—my little brother and I were still in elementary school. Dad said he had a surprise for us. We got excited and asked him what it was. He pulled an envelope out of his shirt pocket (he always kept things in his shirt pocket) and opened it. There were a few small, unrecognizable slips of paper, and it took us a few seconds to figure it out. He asked if we wanted to go to a Mets game that weekend. I didn't even know people did that. I watched the Mets on television every night, and I suppose I recognized that there were people in the stadium watching the game, but I just thought they were special or something. The thought of actually attending a live game seemed inconceivable.

Needless to say, I was elated. The next couple of days dragged on as they always do when you're looking forward to something. I couldn't think of anything else. I made a crappy "Let's Go Mets" sign on a piece of computer paper with crayons. I had my Mets t-shirt laid out for days in advance so I wouldn't waste any time that morning. My glove was ready for foul balls I wouldn't catch, and I counted the days, the hours, and the minutes.

    I remember we left early in the morning for the afternoon game. My dad drove, my mother sat in the front seat, and my two brothers and I sat in the back. I remember talking about the lineup with my dad as we drove on the long road that had all the "Exit" signs on it. (I learned later on in life that this was the Long Island Expressway.) He said we had to follow the numbers and watch them get lower. I remember it started to rain.

    Interrupting our conversation about crafting the perfect lineup, my mother noted the rain. I heard what she was saying, but I remember consciously trying to not listen to her threats. I remember looking down at my glove, looking over at my brothers, looking in front of me at my dad driving, and trying to pretend she wasn't there.

My dad kept pointing out the exit signs, trying to preserve our excitement and anticipation as best he could. When we finally reached our exit, my dad told us to look out the window and see if we could see the stadium. I remember how life-sized it looked, how incredibly big and real. It was blue and had giant images of players along the side: a pitcher, a batter, and a squatting catcher, all lit up. It was the most amazing thing I had ever seen. Certainly different from what we saw on our 32" Zenith—plus, they rarely showed the outside of the stadium on television. It was a lot to take in, and I savored every detail. There it was, Shea Stadium, right there, and I was going to sit next to my dad and watch the Mets play. The rain had slowed to a drizzle.

When we pulled into the parking lot, we had to pass through a little toll booth to pay for parking. My dad rolled (yes, rolled) down his window and asked the elderly lady in the booth if the Mets were going to win today. I thought it was silly, but she played along and said, "Of course!" Honest admission: I still do that every time I go to a game.

We parked, grabbed our coats and the bags full of snacks my mother insisted on bringing because apparently we'd have to be fuckin morons to pay for food or drinks at the game. I didn't care, though. I ignored her for much of the day. I was somehow able to put her out of my head and stay focused on what mattered. It was a special occasion—my first ever Mets game—and I couldn't let her ruin it.

As we walked toward the stadium, I noticed everyone was wearing Mets shirts and Mets hats and Mets jerseys and holding signs and big foam fingers. I kept trying to see people's backs to see the names on their jerseys. There was Gooden and Dykstra and Strawberry and Carter, and I thought it was neat that I recognized them. I kept pointing them out to my dad. He smiled and directed us toward our entrance gate. Through the whole ride there, my dad kept telling me to wait for the tunnel. I didn't know what he meant, so I went along with it. He kept saying it was the best part. He repeated it as we approached the gate. "Wait for that tunnel, I'm tellin' ya'."

You know what? He was right. It was the best part.

We walked through the gate. I couldn't get over how big the place was, how there was blue and orange everywhere and gigantic posters of famous Mets players. I can still feel the excitement; I feel my heart picking up its pace as I'm writing this. We got our tickets checked, and then we rode up what seemed like a hundred escalators, allllll the way up to the top. I was afraid of heights, but somehow it didn't bother me on that day. We turned a corner and started walking. I remember the smell of hot dogs. People were eating peanuts and cracker jacks and drinking soda and beer out of tall cups and walking earnestly and talking and smiling. There were signs above us every few feet that had numbers on them, and my dad said that we had to find the one that matched what it said on our tickets. It took forever, but it was worth every second. My mother trailed behind us, saying something about how stupid we were and how we'd probably get lost if she wasn't behind us to supervise. Whatever. We finally found it, the sign with our numbers. We got to the tunnel.

    I remember walking through that little corridor-the tunnel, coming out and seeing it all in front of me. The view of the field from that perch was a sight I will never forget. I can close my eyes this very second and see it all. It was incredible. The grass in the outfield looked so rich and green and there were men on the infield with rakes and brooms making sure the dirt was just right, and there was a man painting the lines of the batter's box. That white paint looked so fresh and bright, and it stretched all the way down each line until it hit the outfield walls. There were players running and warming-up and some players in the outfield were playing catch and throwing the ball farther than I ever could. The scoreboard was enormous. And that screen! Diamond Vision! What a sight! I looked at the outfield walls. They looked so far away from home plate that I remember thinking it had to be nearly impossible to hit a homerun.

My dad leaned down and pointed.

"Look down there," he said.

There it was: The New York Mets' dugout. I saw the players sitting and standing. I tried to squint to see the names on the backs of their jerseys. I remember spotting Doc Gooden. He was really there. He was standing right there!

"Did you see that?" my dad asked.

I looked toward the outfield where he was pointing. It was the Homerun Apple. It was so cool. I remember hoping to see a Met hit a homer so it would go up. There was so much to take in, so much to capture in that moment. It was the happiest I had felt in a really long time. And my dad was right there next to me.

I could have stood there on that little platform at the end of the tunnel and watched the whole game next to my dad. I could have stood there forever. And when I close my eyes during a bad day, or when I need to think of him to get me through something, that's where I go—I stand there, at the end of the tunnel, looking down on that baseball field, standing next to my dad, and I drink it all in.

    The game hadn't even started, and the crowd was already loud. Nothing against Citi Field, but no stadium rocked like Shea Stadium. Planes flew overhead every few innings, and the noise they made was Earth-shattering. We couldn't even talk over them. We walked up a thousand steps and found our red seats way up high in the upper deck. I sat between my two brothers, then it was my mother, and then my dad. I remember I kept leaning forward and looking to see his reactions to what was going on. Every now and then, he looked over at me and smiled. It was one of the greatest memories of my life.

    The rain started to pick up around the third or fourth inning. It didn't bother me, but I did start worrying. A monsoon wouldn't have bothered me that day. The Mets were losing, but I didn't care about that, either. (We were used to that sort of thing.) Five innings in, and I still couldn't get over the fact that I was with my dad at Shea Stadium watching the New York Mets.

My mother stood up and said it was time to go. She said it "wasn't necessary" to sit in the rain and get soaked like "fuckin idiots." We got up and walked down the steps and through the tunnel and down the escalators and out of the stadium and through the parking lot to our car. It was only the fifth inning.

My first ever Mets game with my dad, and my mother made us leave in the fifth inning because she didn't want to sit in the rain. They didn't call the game. There wasn't even a rain delay. It was only a drizzle, for God's sake. I truly hated my mother for that. In fact, that was the first time I can consciously remember feeling real hatred for anyone. Go figure it was for my own mother.

Thinking about it now, I see the irony: one of favorite childhood memories was also one of my worst. I had looked forward to it so much— all I wanted to do was watch a game with my dad, and my mother ruined it. She shouldn't have even been there. She seemingly went just for the sake of ruining it. I know it may not seem like much—having to leave a game early. But to me, it was worse than anything she had ever done to me. Yes, it was worse than wearing the diaper and worse than being choked until I pissed myself. It was worse than the wooden spoon that made my ass bleed and worse than the time she made me spend the day alone in the laundry room because I accidentally spilled milk on the kitchen table. It was worse than when she screamed at me in front of everyone in the main hallway of my elementary school because I didn't do my homework because she felt the public embarrassment was necessary. It was worse than the time she held my head under the bathtub faucet until I choked because I said I didn't like the way she washed my hair because the water and shampoo got in my face and eyes and dad did it better. It was worse than when she humiliated me in front of my middle school football team because she told me I had to be home by five for dinner, but practice ran late so she showed up to the field and screamed at me in front of everyone. I already had no friends, and she made me get in the car with my uniform on and then made me quit the team because practices ran too late. It was worse than not being allowed to play any sports in high school because practices ran too late and sports were a waste of time. It was worse than the time she hit me over the head with a glass salad dressing bottle. It was worse than all of that shit. Much worse. And it's a memory I can't shake. Granted, people have experienced far more traumatic events during childhood, but that one stuck with me.

      Hatred is a strong word, and one I don't use often. Truthfully, I can't think of another human being I feel that way about. I'm not proud of it. I'm not proud that I hate my mother. People are often judged by how they treat and regard their mothers, but what can I say? Nobody is perfect. I have hatred. A lot of it. And it's not going anywhere.

Chapter 13

The glass salad dressing bottle was the last time my mother hit me. It wasn't the first time by any means, and it was far from being the worst, but it was surely the last. Thinking back, it wasn't even that big of a deal. It sounds worse than it was. She didn't smash the bottle over my head like you see in the movies, when one guy breaks a beer bottle over another guy's head. She didn't come at me with a running start or spool up a back swing. She got up from the table, upset at me for something I can't remember, and bopped me on top of my head with the bottle as nonchalantly as if she had asked for the bottle of soda to be passed. So I can't explain why it set me off. I don't know why I reacted the way I did, but I'm glad I did it. It took me sixteen years to do it, but I finally stood up for myself.

To this day, it's not something I'm good at. No, that's too complimentary. I'm horrible at it. Perhaps sixteen years of consistent training takes its toll. So as an admitted consequence,

I'm not a confrontational person; the mere thought of it makes me uneasy. I'm not saying I don't have my beliefs, because I do, and I do stick to them, but mostly internally. I know that probably doesn't count for much. I find myself conceding in general conversations because it's easier than quarreling. It's simpler to agree with someone and then dismiss their contentions after I've walked away. Besides, everyone is entitled to an opinion. I will, on a rare occasion, stand my ground, but I always do so with uneasy footing. It's a flaw I clearly recognize in myself, and it is said that admitting an inadequacy is the first step toward solving it. Let's just say it's a work in progress.

    Getting back to the salad dressing bottle… I suppose that evening, I had had enough. Everyone has a breaking point, even those who shy away from conflict. And I've worked hard to lengthen my anger fuse, but that night it blew quickly. We were sitting in the kitchen having dinner, just a normal evening, and something ignited her. I don't even remember what it was this time, and that's the truth (not like she ever needed a reason). She got up from her seat, grabbed the bottle (which was odd in and of itself because we never ate salad) and walked toward me. She smacked me on the top of the head with the butt of the bottle and continued walking toward the sink as if nothing had happened. But something did happen. Something triggered in me that I had never felt before, and it's only recurred a handful of times since. I exploded from my chair and started screaming. I lost it. I suppose there's no specific reason why certain things stick in your head like glue and other things become blurry and eventually fade away, but this is a vivid memory. Among other things I spurted, I told her that I hated her. I told her that if she ever touched me again, I'd fuckin' break her in half and end her life. I'd end her if she ever touched me again. Yep, fuse officially blown. I actually threatened to kill my own mother. She didn't respond. I walked out of the kitchen, leaving behind an unfinished plate, a half-full cup of soda, and a table full of agape mouths. I went up to my room, closed my door, and sat on my bed thinking about what had just happened. What I had just said. Why I said it and how I felt. And you know what? I felt pretty damn good about myself. Not because I threatened to murder another person (for the written record, I would never actually kill anyone), but because I finally said something. I didn't know what effect it would have on our future conflicts, but that wasn't my concern or focus. I stood up for myself, and that made me happy.

Chapter 14

The sixteen years I endured before the salad dressing bottle weren't good. I often hear people reminisce about cherished childhood memories, and it's a conversation I habitually remove myself from. I'm not envious, nor am I bitter; I just don't have much to contribute to the discussion. If I have to, I'll share something, but I'll downplay whatever the story is, gloss over unwanted details, and lace it with enough humor and sarcasm to thoroughly conceal any actual emotion or hurt or pain. No need for any of that. Nobody wants to hear it and I don't want to say it.

I'll admit I have enough resulting psychological issues to keep Freud busy for a semester or two, but I maintain my position on complaining.

Being a teenager. Yeah, that sucks for a lot of people and for a lot of different reasons. Some kids lack athleticism and suffer socially as a result. Some kids are fat, others are kinda stupid or fully stupid, lots of kids endure nasty divorces and f'd up households with crazy and/or unfit parents, and there are those who deal with tragedies most adults couldn't fathom, let alone handle with poise and clarity of mind. I am cognizant of that, I assure you. That's why I hate pity. I hate when people walk around showing the world their sob stories with giant "Woe Is Me" posters hanging from their necks. Where does that get you? How long do you ride that? There's a point when feeling sorry for yourself becomes counter-productive and you need to move on. Otherwise, what is your goal? To wake up years later, having wasted your life complaining and making excuses and not being where you want to be or who you could have been? No, thanks. You can keep the pity. Feeling sorry for myself is a waste of time. There are those who deal with far worse than I have ever been through, and they don't ask for or need sympathy. They take the hits, and they keep fighting. Those are the people I admire, and that's what I have aspired to be—a DOer, not a complainer.

Here comes a (purposeful, I promise) tangent: Rocky. One of my favorites. Frankly, it should be on everyone's favorite list. (Okay, that's just my opinion; it's not a fact.) That series got me through a significant portion of my childhood. My dad and I would watch them whenever they were on television (as long as they didn't interfere with the Mets). And luckily, they were often on some movie channel played in succession. We loved Stallone and we especially loved the training scenes toward the end when Rocky was getting ready for the big fight. The music. His muscles. The nervous tension as we awaited the fight (even though we've seen it a thousand times and we knew Rocky was going to win). Then, of course, came the fight. Rocky would be down and seemingly out, exhausted, bloody, and bruised. And just when you thought it was over, when it seemed like there was no hope... well, you know the rest.

Those movies were amazing. Rocky: a true cinematic icon. In 2006, Sylvester Stallone made a dream of mine come true by bringing one of my childhood heroes back to the big screen. Here I was, an adult, sitting in a movie theater with my little brother, and watching Rocky do it again. The same kick-ass music. Even more veins popping out of his thick, vascular forearms. It was a piece of childhood brought back to life, and we loved every minute of it. My favorite scene, though, wasn't the fight. It wasn't even the training montage. (I still have the soundtrack as my workout mix—don't judge.) Of course, those scenes were cool, and I sat on the edge of my seat air-boxing along with him and breaking into a sweat while my brother laughed at me, but my favorite part was the conversation he had with his son outside his restaurant. If you've seen the movie, you know exactly what I'm talking about. I have his entire speech blown up on a poster in my room. You don't have to be a prize-fighter to relate. His point has stuck with me since, and anytime I catch myself feeling about feeling bad for myself or when I feel like I'm up against the ropes about to collapse and take the loss, I close my eyes and hear his words.

"It ain't about how hard you hit. It's about how hard you can get hit and keep moving forward. How much you can take and keep moving forward. That's how winning is done!"

Truer words have never been spoken. I know it's a movie, but there is much we can learn from the world of fiction, especially from someone like Mr. Balboa. Yes, I've taken hits. But we all have. That's what makes it a fight. You can't win all the time. You can't be the one dishing out the hits all the time. Failure is a necessary part of life; in fact, it may be one of life's most powerful and useful lessons. Failure is provocation. It's motivation. Or it should be, anyway. Sometimes life knocks you flat on your ass, even when you can't defend yourself. And life doesn't care if you're old or a kid, rich or poor, black or white, blessed or cursed. It doesn't care if your parents blew smoke up your ass for years and made you think you were perfect or if they did their best to screw you up. Life hits and it hurts. Some people have jaws like glass and enjoy playing the victim. They like not having to try their hardest because hey, guess what happened in my life that made me this way. It's not my fault and there's nothing I can do. Then there are people like Jackie Robinson who showed us all that complaining doesn't get you anywhere. (Just read Randy Pausch's thoughts on this—he can explain it better than I ever could.) There are people who spend their lives in wheelchairs and never bitch about it, people who lose their homes to fires or natural disasters and then pick up the pieces and move on. People who have to bury their children but find a way to keep living. The point is, no matter how bad you think your life is, someone has it worse. Someone is having a shittier day than you. Someone out there would wish to have your problems. So suck it up, take the punches, and do whatcha' gotta' do.

 Thanks for the advice, Rocky.

Part II: Try to Keep Your Hands Up

Chapter 15

By the time I was about fifteen or sixteen, the junk food thing had taken its toll on me and I got to see the number 200 on our bathroom scale. Not bad for a 5'7" kid with zero muscle tone and minimal (okay, basically non-existent) athletic potential. I got up every morning and stretched my size 38 husky pants over my fat ass and wore a loose t-shirt or a baggy sweatshirt to cover the belly that hung nicely over my belt. Picked last in gym class, no doubt. And no, no dates—tough to imagine, I know.

There were a lot of things I wasn't allowed to do. That's just the way it was. Taking the bus, for example. We had buses in Port Jefferson. Big, yellow ones. And would you believe they picked you up near your house and brought you right to the school? They even brought you home after school. How convenient. Not for me, they weren't. Mother didn't approve of the time the bus came and thought the ride home took too long, so she insisted on driving me every day. Every single day. The bus stop was about a half-mile from our house, which would have given me at least a little time for myself (and it could have slightly helped my weight problem), but instead, I would sit in the back of her white Mercedes Benz (confession: I will never—even if I could afford to—buy or lease a Mercedes) and inhale and exhale her smoke all the way to school while she told me fabricated stories about my father. I figured out they were fake by the time I was in middle school—they just didn't add up and became more ridiculous with every repetition. And seeing how she and my dad conducted themselves solidified my hypothesis that she was full of it. The way home was the same thing. I'd sit in the back and try to tune her out. Thankfully, it wasn't a long ride. Her argument that the bus ride would take too long—I thought that was funny. I would have loved a nice, long bus ride.

But no buses, and no field trips, either. Port Jefferson, if you're not familiar, is a quaint, relatively affluent town on the north shore of Suffolk County, Long Island, and the school rarely spared any expense. In elementary school, the whole class (as small as it was) went to Frost Valley for an overnight trip. In middle school, there were two trips: one to Boston and the other to Washington, DC. But the best, by far, was saved for last. Senior year. The class trip to Disney World in Orlando, Florida. People still talk about that trip. How even the plane ride was fun. How cool the teachers were. The friendships created and solidified, the enchanting memories that will never fade, the experience of a lifetime. It's another topic I habitually avoid. Mother didn't trust the school teachers or administrators to be in charge of my safety or well-being, so I stayed home for all of them. Apparently, all the teachers and administrators had ulterior motives and would likely lose track of me, deliberately leave me somewhere, molest me or abuse me in some horrible way, and see to it that I never returned safely. Thank goodness for the safety and sanctity of my home. It was nice hearing about all the trips and trying to create plausible reasons for my absence when the unavoidable (yet completely understandable) questions were asked.

If you haven't figured it out yet, I am a fan of irony. I see humor in ironic situations. Here was my mother "protecting me" from the outside world. She didn't believe anyone else was capable of providing care and safety. And while she constantly stressed the importance of school, she disallowed any aspect of it that might have been enjoyable. So, school, and anything associated with it, was reduced to a place to go and spend some hours not being at home. That's all it was and all I knew.

Chapter 16

I was not a good student. No sense in lying about it. I eked my way through four years of high school with straight C+s, knowing that the option of going away to college was never on the table. I'm not proposing I would have tried harder if I knew there was a chance of getting away, but perhaps it would have been some provocation to give a small crap. I couldn't go away. According to mother, "it wasn't necessary" and "there were perfectly good schools close to home" and "anyone who went away to school was a fuckin moron." So from the start of my freshman year when people around me sprinkled the word "college" into occasional conversations, I knew where I stood. And during the latter part of junior year and all through senior year when the word took over many a conversation, I performed my usual Houdini act and split. My destiny was set: after high school, I would, without option or discussion, go to Suffolk County Community College in Selden and remain living at home.

Now don't get me wrong—I think SCCC is a great school, and if taken seriously, it can pave the way to just about anywhere. And if I had to do my life over again, with what I know about student loans and ridiculously inflated price tags, and the first years of any collegiate institution being virtually academically identical, I would go there again. But I would have appreciated an option. I know there is much to be said for going away—it's a valuable experience that teaches a young adult to grow up, gain independence, make decisions, and learn responsibility and accountability. It's a social learning experience as well. So I understand the allure of going away, and I'm well aware of how many kids do it to distance themselves from their parents for various reasons. I needed that distance, too, so I filled my non-school hours with work. Perhaps it wasn't a perfect situation, but I made the best of it.

  Okay, back to high school. I didn't put forth an effort because, frankly speaking, I didn't care to. I saw no purpose in busting my ass for an A when doing the bare minimum got me a C. I was smart enough to get the C without working hard, so that was that. Extra effort. For what? For whom? The only reason to try at all was to avoid hearing crap when I got home. But I'll tell ya', even that gets old after a while. When I was in middle school, back when I sort of cared about academia, I occasionally bombed a quiz or a test (I'm only human) and got to face mother's wrath as a result. One failed quiz lead to hours of incessant yelling and name-calling and being mercilessly berated. What does that teach you? To work hard enough not to hear your mother's screaming? No, thanks. You can keep jabbing and punching; I'll stand here and take it.

    When I screwed up my grades in high school, my dad tried his best to reason and parent. By the time I was in tenth-eleventh grade, my mother had—I can only suppose—given up on me and my grades and decreased her frequency of flipping out. I started distancing myself from her, basking in the freedom provided by a couple of friends with cars and licenses. In hindsight, I understand that by not being in the house, I had effectively removed a once-forced audience. Because she saw no opportunity to lecture me about my father and her expansive selection of stories, she saw no point in interacting with me. And trust me—there was ZERO complaining about that on my end. The less time I spent interacting with her, the better. So, I had no complaints or problems with her having given up on and virtually ignoring me once I stopped fulfilling her needs.

      My dad didn't give up on me, though. And his pedagogy was drastically different. He had a steady-handed, predictable approach to me and my studies. When progress reports and report cards (yes, they were printed on real paper and sent through the mail way back when) landed on my dad's desk, he'd have me come into his office and we'd sit across from each other and he'd talk to me about the value of hard work. About the value of putting forth a solid effort. About how it wasn't *what* I was learning that mattered, but how I learned it and how learning how to learn was crucial for what would come later. It all sounds logical. That's what school is for—to practice taking in unfamiliar information and making sense of it. It's about learning to problem solve and developing a work ethic. It's about developing a sense of independence and an understanding of responsibility and commitment, time management and perseverance. It made sense, and it was spoken through a calm mouth and with a normal conversational volume. And looking back, I can only imagine his concealed frustration in having to hit the repeat button so often. It's not that I didn't understand or agree with what he was saying. It just wasn't enough to motivate me. I suppose motivation must come from within. And it wasn't coming from within.

  Remember when I told you how my dad woke up between five and six AM, worked until five PM, and often went back to work after that unless the Mets game was on? Well, it wasn't an accident that we lived in affluent Port Jefferson or that mother drove a Mercedes Benz or that I always had new clothes (albeit husky ones) or that there was always food on our table (nutritious or not) or that we got nice, expensive presents on Hanukkah. You see, without saying anything about it, my dad was *showing* me the value of hard work every day of my life. He was a living example of why working hard was important, why sacrificing and prioritizing were necessary. He did what he had to do to make sure my siblings and I had a nice home and went to a safe school. He tried so hard to teach me these valuable life-lessons every single day. I was just too blind to get it and too stupid to apply it. That's a depressing reality I have to live with. I'm not proud of it.

Nevertheless, there I sat. I sat in his office where he worked tirelessly, without sick days or personal days or mental health days or extended vacations, where he spent countless hours making sure his family was provided for. And the hours were countless—I never heard him speak of hours per week or calling it quits early here and there. The man worked his ass off and would have been satisfied if I had done half that. So I sat there, time after time, day after day, and I listened to him tell me about work ethic. I listened to him, over and over again, talk to me from behind the desk he never took vacations from. I listened to him explain the value of going the extra mile as we sat there in our enormous basement in our gigantic five-thousand square-foot house in an elite neighborhood on the north shore of one of the most expensive communities on Long Island, and I did nothing.

Perhaps I wasn't the only one up against the ropes with frustration and seemingly unavoidable defeat. I'm sorry, Dad.

Chapter 17

Ever hear of Belle Terre? Unless you live in Suffolk County, New York, probably not. Belle Terre is a tiny community within and sharing a zip code with Port Jefferson. Sharing a zip code means the post office considers it Port Jefferson, but the habitants of this tiny sector prefer the exclusivity of such a distinguishing label. It's a private section with its own police and its own country club and its own rules. There's an enchanting entrance gate. And when you pass through this gate and enter this kingdom in your luxury vehicle of choice, you instantly find yourself in a magical land where the houses are more extravagant than what you see on television, where the taxes reach astronomical proportions and give the residents something to playfully bitch about while they play golf, where the cars are never dirty but the secrets are, where the noses are perpetually angled toward heaven even though the behavior points the other way, and where the sense of entitlement is as inflated as the egos. My hometown. No bitterness, I promise.

Okay, let's pause for a second. I spent the first part of this story telling you about some of the abuse I suffered as a kid. That might have painted the picture of a rough childhood, but it was only rough in parts. Allow me to clarify: we didn't go hungry. We didn't wear dirty clothes (except for the ones I pissed in). We didn't have to want for anything. Money was never a problem, even though my parents argued about it to no end. Yes, my childhood was tough, but there are millions of children who have it much worse. Sure, my mother was a raging psychotic who suffered from various mental impairments but refused counseling or treatment, and sure, I have my own personality disorders as delightful parting gifts, and no, I haven't spoken to her in I-don't-know-how-many years, and yes, I wish my childhood was a little less colorful. But there are those who have it worse, much worse. Don't think I have overlooked or forgotten that for a second. I know how fortunate I am to have what

I have, what I had, and to be who I am. That's why you can keep the pity and the sympathy. Give it to someone who needs and deserves it. After all, I'm still here, aren't I?

Back to the story. Where was I? Oh yeah, high school and life among the rich and richer. So after my dad would share his wisdom and sensibilities that I was too stupid to listen to, I got to deal with mother. Only in the beginning of high school, though. By around my junior year, I imagine she figured out that I was no longer impressed and finally started to leave me the hell alone. But before that, I still had to deal with her.

Not that I'm trying to gloss over it, but let's spare some of the specifics for the sake of time and combine them into one generally accepted scene that played out routinely and with occasional creative variations. She'd look at my report card, scream curses, call me clever names, threaten that I would "rot in hell," use it as a chance to make fun of my weight and occasional spurts of acne, explain how I was undoubtedly a product of my piece-of-shit father and deserved a seat in hell next to him (at least we'd be sitting together), threaten to take away any and every possession, and then come up with some purposeless task like the time she made me copy my entire history textbook into a notebook because she was sick of me being "a fuckin moron who couldn't study on my own." Like I said, there were occasional variations. Nobody likes stagnation, right? So I got to write my vocabulary words a thousand times, I had the pleasure of watching all of my books be thrown into the trash and was wished good luck in trying to explain to my teachers why I didn't have any books. I guess it was during junior year, after I threatened to kill her after the salad dressing bottle, that I (forgive my language—I'm blaming my upbringing) told her to fuck off. I had had enough of her garbage and perhaps she realized that I was getting too old for it anyway. So through my senior of high school I went, seldom saying a word to mother. It was better that way.

Senior year was—if I'm being forthright—a good time for me. Really, it was. Barely speaking to or interacting with mother was a solid plus. I had lost weight because I had finally taken control of my own eating, I started working out thanks to my older brother (who also dealt with perpetual weight and body fat issues) kicking my ass and making me lift weights with him, and I started caring about how I dressed, how my hair looked and how clean it was, and how I smelled—which was accompanied by the wonderful discovery of deodorant and (reaching for the stars here) cologne.

It was also during this time, and quite likely due to going to the gym together, that my older brother and I became close. We share the same birthday, believe it or not. Six years apart to the day. We had a rough stint as kids (stint—that's the wrong word; we fought for over a decade until I turned seventeen or so and stopped pissing him off), but making him proud has always been in the back of my mind. Brothers fight, I get it. And so we did. But, as brothers do, we got past it, moved on, and grew up. (Remember that, Alex and Matt.) My older brother is my idol. He's the kind of person who does whatever has to get done. He does it well, and he doesn't complain. That's why I look up to him. That's how he was when he and I worked together at the gas station where he was a manager and I was a fuel distribution engineer (I worked the full-serve pumps), when we lifted weights together, and that's how he'll always be. Meticulous and careful and thorough. He's a hard worker, just like my dad was. He's an expert homeowner who somehow knows how to fix anything and everything, he's an attentive father and a dedicated husband, and he's the funniest uncle a kid could ever ask for. And as I'm writing this, I realize how he reminds me a lot of my dad, which could be part of the reason I admire him so much. He's a good man and one heck of a big brother. He's the kind of person who would stop whatever he was doing if you needed help. My dad was that way, too. I guess that's where my brother got it from. He's always ready with a warm hug, a contagious belly laugh, or a good ass-kicking whenever I need.

So, there I was, enjoying my senior year. My circle of three friends grew to double digits, which meant I had things to do on the weekends and during the week. No, I didn't have a curfew because mother didn't care where I was or what I was doing and because my dad knew me well enough to know I wasn't into drinking or doing drugs. (That's the truth—I didn't drink in high school and I've never done drugs.) Going out during the week was great because it got me out of my house and gave me a sense of purpose and belonging and acceptance. Spending time with my older brother was awesome, too. Until I reached this not-annoying age, I was rarely included in his social outings. But I remember him inviting me to go out with his friends, to go for a ride in his car, to start going to the gym with him. That felt really good, and it sure meant a lot to me. I'm so thankful that he and I have formed a friendship that we continue today. And sharing a birthday is pretty cool, too.

To top off my illustrious senior year of high school—get ready for this—I had a girlfriend. That's right. More than a few friends, a fun job, an awesome big brother, and a girlfriend. She was cute as could be and fun and sweet and I fell in love for the first time. It's ok, you can go ahead and say it: *Awww*.

We dated for a long time. Well, a long time for high schoolers. Our relationship lasted over a year and took me into my first semester at college. She was younger than I was, still in high school, and our path differentials got the best of us. It didn't last, I broke it off, we were both heartbroken (I know, it happens), and that was that. But it was amazing while it lasted and she'll always hold a special place in my heart.

Senior year. It was a fun time. I didn't stress over college nonsense because I knew my options were limited, I didn't worry about my grades because I knew a community college only required that I graduate high school, and my time was divided between hours at the station, hanging out with my friends and my brother, and spending time with my girlfriend. I was working out and feeling good about being me. Senior year—I won that round.

Chapter 18

College. That's where I went after high school. Our society dictates that sort of thing these days. If you don't go to college, you won't be successful. When you graduate high school, whether you have a determined path toward professionalism or are aimless and clueless and useless, you go to college. I find this concept particularly disturbing. I know plenty of people who never went to college and are doing just fine. I also know people—as I'm sure you do—who went through the motions and the expense of college, even got degrees, and do absolutely nothing with them besides pay back student loans and regret not joining the workforce years earlier. College isn't for everyone, and not enough people recognize the ugliness and danger of that stigma. But off to college I went. Why not?

Suffolk Community College: A hopeful educational institution brimming with potential—new faces and new classes and new opportunities. A chance for someone to redefine himself, to rid himself of a previous reputation and construct a new one. A place to build confidence and a future. Or something like that. I didn't know what the hell I was doing there.

    I knew all my friends from senior year were hours away, I knew my girlfriend was now my ex-girlfriend and I would go back to spending my weeknights and weekends alone, and I had trouble making new friends because I didn't want to be there in the first place. It was also because (okay, might be an excuse) a commuter college doesn't lend itself to a communal environment; every person comes and goes on a different, personalized schedule revolving around jobs, and socializing more than a few words outside a building before or after a class was about all I wanted or could handle.

    I found solace at work. I liked working because I saw value in it, unlike my hours spend in high school or college classrooms. If I worked X amount of hours, I got X amount of money at the end of the week. Simplicity. Predictability. The guys in the shop would leave by six, full-serve would close around eight (even though I sometimes closed it a wee bit earlier), and after that I locked the door, sat down with the homework I wasn't going to do, ate my dinner, played my music, and relaxed the evening hours away. After nine-ish, traffic slowed, and patrons were sparse, and I was alone with my thoughts. I enjoyed the solitude. I enjoyed the freedom and the quiet. And I certainly enjoyed not being at home and, of course, getting paid for the privilege. By the time I got home shortly after eleven, everyone was sleeping, so it was a win-win.

My older brother was the manager, and he's the one who got me the job. Working with him was a pain in the ass at times (working with family can get like that), but I enjoyed spending the time with him. I was also amazed watching him work. He seemed to have one speed: fast. Things needed to get done, and he did them. It was also cool being pulled into another social circle. Because he was liked and respected, the guys treated me well, too. Another thing to thank my brother for.

I saw no reason to change jobs, as I was treated quite well by a boss who is, to this day, the best boss I've ever had. As long as you did your job, you had his respect. He was an effective leader who saw the best in people and was therefore able to construct and conduct a productive staff. And he was down-to-Earth. Yeah, he owned the business and made a lot of money, I'm sure, but he always seemed to get it. By this time, I had developed an interest—like my older brother—in cars, and took note of what people drove. I always appreciated my boss's succession of cars and how he went from driving a piece of crap to something decent to something nice to something pretty nice to something fancy to something really fancy (but still within the realm of normal). I guess I saw something in it. Something along the lines of what my dad had tried to tell me all those years. Here was a guy, like my own father, who owned his own business and worked his ass off and reaped the rewards of his own relentless efforts. He wasn't just handed success. He faced risks, he made sacrifices, and he stayed focused. He prioritized.

He was all about his family and he worked to provide for them. I respected this man immensely for this, and I'm thankful that he and I are still friends to this day. I've always looked up to him, I've always tried to make him proud, and I've always been thankful for what he gave me—whether he realized it or not. I also feel like even though my job wasn't the most prestigious or financially fulfilling, I was still working instead of sitting on my ass all day, and I always hoped that would somehow make my dad proud. It wasn't a lot, but it was something.

Part III: Get Knocked Down

Chapter 19

I've always been a routine-oriented fella (just in case that wasn't clear yet). A creature of habit, as they say. I like ritualistic behavior. There's predictability. There's comfort. Waking up at the same time, following the same exact steps as the day before, and knowing exactly what to do next and what's to follow. No surprises. Even though I was thrown by the start of college in all its newness, I had once again established a workable routine. I continued going to the gym early in the morning with my brother. Getting up early is not fun; getting my head off the pillow is the hardest part. But I like the way I feel for the rest of the day. I've already accomplished something that others are unwilling to do. Plus, there's the added benefit of controlled weight and body fat, which works wonders in building and maintaining confidence. It's a habit I still continue today. There aren't too many people in the gym at 5AM, so I can work out quickly and efficiently before starting my day.

After working out, I'd head to SCC for a morning full of classes. I liked morning classes because, as I discovered, the clientele for an 8AM English 101 course was comprised of people who, like me, went to work after school and didn't have time to smoke cigarettes and didn't give a crap about showing off their snazzy outfits in the student center. A quick bite to eat and perhaps some coffee, and then I enjoyed the serenity of the evening shift at the gas station. By the time I got home around 11:15, everyone was sleeping and the house was quiet. My routine was productive and predictable, just the way I like it.

It happened during my first year of college, on a rare weekday when I didn't have to go to work. I finished my classes, popped into the local deli that had surprisingly good egg white sandwiches, and went home in an attempt to find some relaxation. Our house had an odd setup, and because mother didn't allow us to have keys, we entered and exited through the garage. There was a doorbell stationed between the two oversized doors, and once inside the garage, there was a door that led to the basement where my dad's office was. When I got home, I strolled into his office, thankful not to see mother there, and sat down at one of his vacant desks. This, too, was a routine. Whenever I came home, I'd stop into his office for a chat. We'd catch up on the Mets, talk about cars or my job, or joke about my dating life. He'd sip his coffee and talk over his reading glasses that rested comfortably on the end of his nose.

    When I walked in that afternoon, he was on the phone (nothing unusual about that), so I sat quietly after grabbing something to drink from his fridge. His pot of coffee still had enough for about a cup, and he had news radio playing lightly from the corner by the window. There were a few desks in his office, each serving a different, yet defined purpose. Some were for computer work, others for paper-driven tasks. And I'll never forget the large one against the back wall that was designated for stuffing envelopes. When asked what my dad did for a living when I was in elementary school, I remember responding the only way I could: "My dad stuffs envelopes." I can appreciate the innocence and naiveté, and my dad often corroborated its humor. After all, it did occupy much of his time and provided, I can only assume, some type of therapeutic respite. I remember sitting there that day looking at the piles of letters and stacks of envelopes, thinking about the evenings he had cleverly tricked my brothers and me into doing slave labor by offering a prize (that didn't actually exist) to whomever stuffed more.

      I was keeping quiet so as not to disturb his call, and I promise I wasn't listening to his conversation on purpose, but something caught my attention. I quickly surmised that he wasn't speaking to a client. His tone was different, not as confident and prepared as usual. There was a noticeable discomfort, even fear in his voice; completely atypical, I assure you. I couldn't help but listen.

For the previous few months, my dad had been experiencing an odd, inexplicable pain in his midsection. It seemingly had no correlation to anything he ate or drank, but mostly happened at night, and it was affecting his sleep. I only knew about it because I overheard his conversation with one of my older brothers a few weeks earlier. There was no complaining in his voice; only matter-of-fact statements and understandable concern. I caught the tail end of this phone call and had to assume what the person on the other line was saying.

"Yes, I'm sitting down."

"So it is cancer?"

"Pancreatic."

"Can I ask you something? Am I going to die?"

Chapter 20

No, I don't remember the rest of the conversation. I don't remember anything else that happened after that, either. I don't remember what classes I sat in that morning, I don't remember what the weather was like, I don't remember what goddamn day it was. I'll tell you what I do remember though. I remember seeing my father cry for the first time in my life. He got up from his desk. He walked over to me, and I stood up. He hugged me tighter than he ever had. He said he didn't want to die. And he cried. My father cried. On my shoulder. And there was nothing I could say or do but cry myself.

It was surreal. My worst fear as a child was my dad dying. I remember having nightmares about him leaving. About not seeing him anymore. About having to live alone with mother. It couldn't happen. I couldn't be left with only my mother. My dad was my hero, and he couldn't die. No way. It didn't make sense.

The unfortunate truth, that I'm sure anyone can admit, is that it never makes sense. Why do the healthiest people contract deadly diseases and those who are not health-conscious live well into old age and die of natural causes? How does cancer choose its targets? How does God—for those who believe in his existence—choose who stays and who goes, and when and how? How does a guy who maintained the same weight since high school, who never drank as much as a six-pack of alcohol in his whole life, who lived through the 60s and 70s without ever touching drugs, who somehow fit in a multi-mile walk every day, get cancer? How does a woman who smoked a pack and a half of cigarettes every day since she was thirteen never develop lung cancer or respiratory issues, but her kid suffered through asthma until he was twenty? No, it doesn't make sense. None of it does. It never has and it never will. There aren't answers. None that will satisfy, anyway. There is no logic behind who gets what or how or when you have to say goodbye to someone. "Everything happens for a reason" sounds nice and all, but doesn't offer any tangible solace for those left behind. Death is a part of life, and no matter how much we love someone, tomorrow is no guarantee. That's a life lesson I had to learn the hard way.

Chapter 21

Now, just to clarify a critical point, I'm not suggesting that one type of cancer is "better" or "worse" than another, nor am I proposing that any of cancer's vast categories are forgiving or easy for the patient and those who love and care for him/her. Anyone who has ever dealt with cancer in any capacity knows and understands the horrors of it. The un-knowing. The battle between hope and fear. The way you allow yourself to feel faith and believe that it will get better while you watch your loved one endure torturous treatments and life-altering prognoses, wondering if and when life will ever again be recognizable. You stay up at night contemplating how you could ever live without. You start praying even though you've never been the praying type. You cry, even though you're not a crier. Cancer is random, it's unforgiving, and all forms of it carry a degree of terror.

All I am saying about pancreatic cancer, specifically, is that it is particularly devastating because it presents virtually no symptoms, is nearly impossible to detect, and because by the time it has been diagnosed, it has progressed in its stages toward fatality, often rendering conventional treatments futile and reducing optimistic goals of saving a life down to prolonging the inevitable.

On the phone that day, the doctor told my dad he had roughly six months to live.

How does one digest that information? I often think of that. If I was given that same information, what would I do? It's a dark concept to contemplate, but I'd be lying if I said I never considered it. It might happen someday; in fact, it's likely because studies suggest there is a hereditary link for pancreatic cancer. So many logistical things would have to be taken care of and ironed out, that I wonder if I would have time to even feel sorry for myself. How would I tell my family and ensure the message isn't misconstrued or embellished as one party relays information to another? How would I face everyone at family gatherings knowing I am the one bringing sorrow and despair to what should be a celebratory occasion? What would I tell work? Would I continue working? How could I just quit? What would I do about my personal items? Would I start throwing stuff out so my loved ones wouldn't have an additional burden to deal with? Would I cancel my dentist appointments? And what about grieving? I wonder how I'd react. Maybe keep it all in and try not to explode? Maybe break down and lose it? I suppose there's no way to really know. But I do know I never heard my dad complain. Not even once. He was upset, surely, and I'd bet he lost sleep to both pain and emotional anguish and fear about what his kids would do without him. But he never complained. He never asked for pity. He didn't proclaim his diagnosis to the world and expect favors, he didn't sit at home and spend hours lost in tears. Nope, not my dad. That's not how he was going to handle this situation. You know what he did? He got up every day and went to work.

Chapter 22

Fortunately, the six-month prognosis wasn't accurate. And for the next few months, other than some doctor appointments, a restrictive diet, and moments of emotional weakness and accompanying breakdowns (on my part, not his), life didn't change much, which was good and bad. On the good side, there was nothing pressing to deal with. My dad was still around, so I wasn't sad or sorrowful. Life went on as normal—nothing drastic. Our house looked and functioned as it always had, and my routine (this sounds so selfish, I know) hadn't been disturbed. It was bad, however, because I refused to prepare myself. I remained conscientiously naïve. Everything was fine, and nothing would ever change. I suppose I could blame immaturity. Yeah, let's go with that. Nonetheless, life went on. My dad maintained his routine, as did the rest of the family. I kept my space from mother who did puzzles on the dining room table in the evening while my dad and I watched the Mets when I wasn't at work.

Mother sat and smoked her cigarettes and started casually drinking white wine and champagne in her celebratory bliss. Like my dad, she was not much of a drinker, ever. But I suppose she found reason to celebrate. Perhaps it was a coping mechanism, but she doesn't deserve that much credit. That's what a normal person might do, and she will never find herself in that category. You know what a normal person doesn't do? A normal person doesn't spend her daylight hours—while her husband works and goes to doctor appointments alone—going through old photo albums with a scissor, cutting my dad's face out of all the family pictures in an attempt to literally and metaphorically erase him from our lives with the convenient assistance of a deadly disease. I know my parents hated each other, and my mother often spoke of how she longed for his death. That didn't help the grieving process, but I wasn't surprised. Even at this point, I had expected her to maintain some level of character, of integrity, of humane decorum, but that was too much to ask. Somehow, thankfully, my siblings and I were able to salvage one or two pictures of him and we ignored the wine bottles that now took up space in the fridge.

During that time, I did what I could to preserve my own routine. I suppose I needed it. I put in my hours at the station, went droningly to my classes, and did my best to keep up with my brother at the gym. And when I wasn't at work, I was sitting with my dad ignoring the tumor-sized elephant in the room as we cheered on our beloved blue and orange.

The doctor appointments became more regular, and my dad eventually underwent chemotherapy and radiation treatment, as could be expected. We all know what that entails. It drained what energy he had, it knocked him on his ass, and it tried to keep him there. I still think it's amazing that he kept his hair. The cancer—and the treatment—took his strength and tried hard to take his spirit as well. I don't mean for this to sound as selfish and as self-centered as it will come out, but it knocked me on my ass, too. And I felt guilty because of it. I wasn't the one being physically tortured day and night. I wasn't the one facing mortality. I wasn't the one who was kept awake at night with agonizing pain and the crippling fear of imminent death. I wasn't the one with cancer. I hated myself for feeling that way, for feeling sorry for myself, for being sad.

    I remember watching my dad go through it all. It can't be easy to maintain a positive demeanor in the face of all that. But he did his best. He kept his routine: he still got up early, still put in a full day of work, arranging his phone calls around his doctor appointments, still spoke to me about the value and importance of a solid work ethic, still slept on a shitty old twin mattress in our basement, and still sat with me to watch the Mets games. He was so tired, I remember. And I knew he felt weak. His appetite was dwindling, his energy all but depleted. But he never complained. He never used any of it as an excuse. Sure, he snuck in a 10-minute "power" nap here and there during the day, but I think that's fair.

Chapter 23

It was around 4:30AM when my cell phone rang on the nightstand next to my bed. It was my sister. As soon as I saw the caller ID, I knew. I answered, she asked if I could come downstairs to let her in through the garage, and she hugged me and confirmed what I already sensed. We woke up my little brother, got dressed, and headed to Mather Hospital. It all happened quickly and painstakingly slowly. It's hard to make sense of it. There were parts that flew by, others that lingered and dragged. It was impossible to process. Still is.

My sister was the one who got the phone call from the hospital because my dad was smart enough to name her his healthcare proxy, knowing that he couldn't have—and shouldn't have—trusted our mother.

From the time my dad was diagnosed, mother took special care to be nastier than usual. She would make comments at dinner about how "he got what he deserved" and how we shouldn't share tableware or glasses because of spread cancer germs. What an asshole.

There was a brief stint before this when my dad—for a reason I honestly don't know—started sleeping upstairs again in the comfort of an actual bed. However, once his sleep started really suffering, causing him to wake in the middle of the night with intense pain, his occasional moan or groan disturbed her, and she told him to go back to the basement because she couldn't sleep through that. And she cranked up the your-father-is-a-piece-of-shit-who-will-rot-in-hell-sooner-than-later talks whenever she got one of us into a room alone. Avoiding her became more habitual with each passing week.

Thinking back, I can't even guess at what her reason was. I know she didn't love or care about my dad, but she claimed (when in public, of course) to be a loving, caring mother. But she had to know that she was pushing us away. She had to recognize that we hated the way she spoke to him and about him and the way she treated us and spoke to us. We resented her.

We hated her. I hated how she treated my dad. I hated how she spoke of him and to him. I hated how she made him feel and how she made me feel. I wished she would have traded places with him. That sounds terrible, I know, but I did promise honesty. I hate her. With every ounce of me and from the deepest depths of me, I hate her. No, I've never gotten over that. I know what it sounds like to hear someone speak of his mother that way, but I hated my mother and I still do and I always will.

Sometime after we arrived at the hospital, mother showed up and avoided us all. We avoided her, too. I remember she kept repeating "it's a mistake," continuing her Broadway performance of the loving, devastated wife for all the nurses and doctors to see. We all kept our distance, and I don't remember seeing her for the rest of the day. It's funny how your memory works sometimes. We—my pregnant sister and her husband, my older brother and his wife, my little brother, and I—took the elevator up, and we entered a small lobby that led to an elongated desk where the nurses sat and looked at computers and monitors. A long, white hallway lead to his room. I remember there were some chairs lined up in the lobby. My oldest brother was there, too, having come up from Florida. We were all there together, all five siblings. All five of us. Together. My oldest brother had already gone into the room to say his final goodbye to our dad, and he said I could if I wanted to, but I didn't have to. I didn't know what to do. A few seconds or minutes later, I stood up and started walking. I'm not sure if it was a conscious decision I made or if it just happened. I didn't know what I was going to see, and I remember being somewhat frightened because of that. I had never seen a real dead body before, certainly not one belonging to someone so close to me. I didn't know what he'd look like or how I'd react. I didn't know if I'd be able to even walk into the room.

September 11, 2001. The day New York will never forget for obvious reasons. That was a dreadful day for so many, a day that will forever be entrenched in our hearts and in our memories. And I feel guilty every year on that day. On that morning, when New York and our country was brought to its knees, my brother drove my dad to the hospital because the pain became too much. We were sitting in his office in our basement, my brother, my dad, and me. News radio was on, discussing the unfathomable events, and we half-listened as we watched my dad settle himself into his chair. He was holding his stomach, having just returned from vomiting in the bathroom, and he asked to be taken to the hospital.

    All of these people were dying at the hands of terrorism, people losing their loved ones without notice or reason, people in a state of utter desperation not even knowing if their mothers or fathers or children or siblings were still alive, and here I was, worrying if my father's drive to the hospital would be a one-way trip. These poor people had no advanced notice, no opportunity to say "I love you" or "goodbye" or "I'm sorry." Every single year, I think of these people, I think of my dad and his final departure to the hospital, and I think of how selfish I am for thinking about me and my problems.

September 23, 2001. About a year and half after my dad's diagnosis. I walked down the long, white hallway and into his hospital room, and I looked at his face for the last time. I sat beside his bed on the windowsill and looked at his peaceful countenance. The swelling and bloating had subsided, and he looked like my dad. I knew this would be the last time I'd ever see him, the last time I'd get to say anything, knowing that he couldn't see me or hear what I had to say. Are there things I wish I would have said to him before he passed? Of course, and that's a regret I have to live with. Things I wish I had said, things I wish he could have seen. I suppose there are many who could understand that feeling, particularly those who lost loved ones on 9/11. But I knew this was the last time I'd ever see him, so I stared at his face without speaking for a moment or two. I cried. And then I spoke.

During the days before, my dad had voluntarily partaken in an experimental treatment, one that offered no guarantees or promises, but one that was worth the risk. The end was nearing, and he knew it, so why not try something that might offer a glimmer of hope? As my dad had explained it, if he was going to go, he wanted to make sure he had exhausted all efforts. The treatment had caused his face to bloat and his speech to slur. It made his hands and feet swell, rendering him almost unrecognizable. The doctors were uncertain as to what ultimately took his life, the cancer or the treatment. My sister, speaking on behalf of her siblings and my dad, rejected their offer for an autopsy because it wasn't necessary. It didn't matter. He was gone, and no report or medical chart or doctor or prayer or tear or nightmare would change that.

I was relieved to see that his face had returned to its familiar form—rounded cheeks, warm complexion, calm yet wrinkled brow. His hair, somehow still mostly full and dark, looked neat as always. His eyebrows, grey and bushy, rested above his closed eyes, and there was no pain or discomfort in his face. He was finally resting. No more worrying about work or paying the bills or fighting an unforgiving disease or battling through a loveless marriage or hoping his kids were raised well enough to stand on their own feet without their father to guide them. Nothing to worry about anymore. His hands were at his sides, and he looked perfectly still as if taking one of his classic power-naps.

    I told him I loved him. I thanked him for being my father. I told him I'd try to make him proud. I kissed his cheek, I said goodbye, and I walked out.

Chapter 24

I don't remember much of what happened the rest of that day or the days immediately after. It all became blurred by intermittent tears, inescapable fear, the hopelessness of being lost, and utter disbelief. I really couldn't process any of it. My worst fear came true. I was living a nightmare.

My dad was dead.

The truth is I felt like an orphan. I had minimal interaction with mother, by design of course, and now without my dad, I truly felt lost. I had time, after his initial diagnosis, to prepare myself, to digest the information, to prepare for his dying. Spending months in denial came back to bite me. I wasn't prepared. And I didn't know what to do.

I remember the funeral home. It was a hot day, one of those humid, steamy ones that lingered as summer came to its end. My tears mixed with sweat as I watched the workers lower his coffin into the ground. I'll never get that image out of my head. They were just doing their job, I understand. But it was painful to watch. When they carried his coffin out of the hearse, my brothers and my sister walked over and took advantage of the opportunity to have one last look at his face. They stood there for a moment, taking it in and perhaps saying a final goodbye. I couldn't do it. I didn't want to. I can't explain why. Years later, I still can't. I stood off to the side and watched them without saying a word. I'm not saying I regret not walking over because I said my goodbye in the hospital room, but I sometimes wonder if I would have done it differently if given the opportunity. But that starts me going down the path of regret because although I told him I loved him the last night I saw him alive, there is still more I could have and should have said. Much more. But there's nothing I can do about it now, so focusing on what can't be is neither healthy nor productive.

We stood there as the sun beat down on us, and we listened to the rabbi say whatever rabbis say when someone dies. I know it's a ritual, but I was only half-listening as I stared at my father's grave, contemplating how final it was. I pictured his face inside that coffin, peaceful and quiet. My family embraced one another while mother dressed in some stupidly inappropriate outfit looked on and pretended to be sad. I glanced at her once or twice, but she didn't deserve any attention. This day wasn't about her. She could sit in the back seat for once and not be seen or heard from.

      I remember my sister speaking through her own tears, expressing her gratitude for having danced with him at her wedding, for having told him the miraculous news of her pregnancy, and how she'd always work hard to honor his wish for his children to stay together. She's the oldest of us—our big sister, and she's the best sister anyone could ever ask for. I know that sounds unnecessarily cheesy, but it's the only way I can describe her. Because mother was the way she was, my little brother and I, in particular, leaned on our sister to be the mother figure. And because she's naturally a caring, empathetic, nurturing woman, our sister helped get us through more than I can ever thank her for. I love her very much, and it made me feel better hearing her speak about dad. It still does, and thankfully, she does it quite often. When we sit around someone's table during a holiday dinner or when we gather to celebrate a birthday, we can count on her to bring up a funny story that we've all heard a million times about dad or reminisce about a memory that makes us all smile. Dad had that habit, too, of repeating the same story over and over, but we never minded because the stories never lost their luster. My sister can tell the same tale as often as she likes, and we'll all listen intently and we'll smile and laugh. She reminds me a lot of him in that way, the way she loves telling stories and the way her cheeks puff up when she tells them. She picked up quite a few habits from my dad; I suppose we all have. I don't often talk about him, an admittedly unhealthy coping mechanism. But she does because it helps her. And somehow that helps me, too.

I guess it's the almost fifteen years that separate us combined with her natural maternal presence, but she's always had the ability to be a big sister when we needed one and a mom when she knew one was needed. She's a remarkable woman, my big sis'. Like my dad, she started her own business and works her tail off to provide for her family. I watch how she is with her two boys, how attentive and focused she is, how dedicated she is to their growth and well-being. And I think that's amazing, especially considering the relationship she had with our mother. (She can write her own book about that.) Every year, on the day of our dad's passing, she texts all of us, checking in and reminding us of his wish that we all remain close and expressing her true gratitude that we have. She's a big part of the reason we have, like the glue that keeps us all in touch and close despite physical distances. And I'm proud that we have stayed so close. My siblings mean the world to me, and that is a lesson I hope Alex and Matt understand one day.

Then my oldest brother spoke. And what he said really hit me. I've always looked up to him, for various reasons, and so whenever he has something to say, I listen. I've always seen him as a guy who has it together. He has this pragmatism about him, a way of not getting riled by inconsequential matters. He's confident, but not cocky. Collected and cool, but not lazy. He has an easy smile, just like my dad did, and a self-awareness I've always envied. And he, too, is all about his kids. You can hear it in his voice when he talks about his boys. He's full of pride and love. He doesn't claim his kids to be perfect, and he has the same sarcastic wit my dad had, but he loves his family and puts them first. And when it was his turn to speak on that morning, I tuned everything else out and felt the brunt of his words. He explained how he had had the opportunity to sit and talk with my dad just days before his passing, to listen to what he had to say, to assure him that his dying wish would be remembered and cherished. He said that dad had something to say about each of us. How proud he was, how much he loved us. My brother went down the line, repeating what my dad had said about every one of his children. Then he got to me.

"Dad was most concerned about you, Lee. He was worried that you didn't have a direction, that you wouldn't know what to do or where to go with your life."

He was right, and I'm sorry.

That was the last thing my father had to say about me. His fourth child, the second-youngest of his children, was lost. I had years full of opportunities to make something of myself, to make him proud of me, to let him go to his grave with the confidence that his boy would be able to stand on his own feet as a man. That's what any father wishes for, right? This guy worked his whole life to surround me with opportunities and advantages, and I had all the time in the world to make something of myself, and I did nothing. The last things my dad said about me were filled with sorrow, despair, frustration, and pain. I was twenty years old, and my father's last thought of me was one of disappointment. I let him down, and that's an excruciatingly painful regret I'll take to my own grave.

Chapter 25

When was the last time you took a good look at yourself in the mirror? I mean really looked deep into your own eyes and assessed yourself, honestly? It's not an easy thing to do, which could be why many people avoid the process. Because it *is* a process. It's not about just recognizing flaws or shortcomings or inadequacies, or even about measuring character. Character, that thing you do when nobody is looking. It's more than that. It's about a willingness to effect change. A readiness to move in a different direction—possibly an uncomfortable one—or to find a direction. It takes maturity and humility. It takes guts.

I faced it that day. It wasn't my intention; not something I meant to do. Certainly not something I wanted to do. I think I was doing it without realizing what I was doing. And here's more of that brutal honesty I promised: I was disgusted by what I saw. Humiliated, even. I found myself face-to-face with a complete jackass (sorry for the informal diction, but it's a real assessment.) A blind, lazy, directionless, purposeless twenty-year-old college dropout who concealed sometimes crippling depression, pumped gas for a couple hundred per week, and gave his own father nothing to be proud of. I don't blame him for that. I wouldn't have been proud of me either.

 That's the part that hurt the most. Still does. The whole time my father was around, I never did anything to make him proud. And I was either too stupid or too arrogant (or both) to listen to what he was trying to tell me. I couldn't see what he was trying to show me. My dad was suffering through chemo and radiation and a permanent (but easy, right doc?) port dug into his torso for facilitated medication infusion, and sleepless nights on a hard, shitty mattress, and incessant vomiting, and lost weight, and no appetite, and no strength, and no energy, knowing that death was imminent. And through all of that, you know what he did? He didn't complain, I can tell you that. Not once did I ever hear that man complain about any of it. He stayed his course as best he could. No, not complaining. Working. That's what he did. He worked. He got up at the same time every morning and showered and shaved and got dressed and went to work. And when he had to spend hours of his day at the doctor to get his treatment, he brought his work with him and asked the nurse if he could use their phone to make calls. He actually used the phone in the hospital to make business calls. He'd spread his notebooks and papers on his bed, and he'd work until the work got done. And when he was dying in a hospital bed in the last weeks of his life while I was busy being a schmuck and not wanting to face reality, he was still working. He showed me what it meant to have a work ethic and why it was important. He shoved that lesson in my face every day of my life, and I didn't get it. That's something I have to live with. That's the thought that keeps me up at night. That's the solid uppercut that knocks me flat on my ass. And it's worse than any other pain I've ever felt.

Part V: Hear the Count 6...7...

Chapter 26

Okay, let's change direction for a minute and talk about something positive. (I need a break.)

I think it's awesome when people get to meet the celebrity of their dreams. It doesn't happen often, but it makes for a cool story to tell. (I promise, I'm going somewhere with this.) A famous movie star you run into at the airport or your favorite athlete happens to be standing behind you on line somewhere. Ever imagine what you'd say if you ever had the chance? Ever think about what that moment would be like?

I have never met my favorite celebrity, and I know the odds are slim that I ever will. That's okay. But I'll tell you this—I know exactly what I'd say to him if I ever got the chance. I'd look him right in his eyes, I'd shake his hand (I figure a hug might be creepy), and I'd say the most genuine, heartfelt "thank you" I've ever spoken.

My father kept a small radio next to his bed in the hospital. He wasn't much for music; news radio and WFAN (the old Mets' Radio Network) were his go-tos. When he couldn't be home on the couch, he listened to the Mets games on his radio. He kept the volume low to avoid disturbing anyone, but those Mets games got him through the evening hours at the hospital after visiting hours had ended. The nurse who was in charge of monitoring my dad said that on the night he died, he was listening to the Mets game. She said that the radio was on, and he was talking about the game with her while she checked his vitals and did whatever nurses do.

I'll tell ya,' it's never easy being a Mets fan. I don't know if we'll ever win a World Series again. And ya' know what? I don't really care. As far as I'm concerned, there were two wins in Mets history that matter more to me than if we won the next ten world championships. One was the night my dad died. The nurse said that she came in late that night after the game was over. She said my dad smiled. He said "The Mets won." And he looked happy. He sat up to adjust himself, and then fell backward onto his pillow. Those were my dad's last words, and that win gave him a final departing smile. And you know what? He deserved it.

I know what you're thinking: What other Mets win could possibly top that or be as monumental? Well, not to worry—I'll tell ya'. The other win happened a few months earlier. It was July 29, 2001. The Mets were playing against the Phillies at good ol' Shea Stadium. It was one of those back-and-forth games, I remember. We had the lead, they tied it up and then went ahead, and the ping-ponging continued. I sat in the left-field stands with my dad and my little brother, and we watched our team. I remember it was early in the game, around the second or third inning, maybe. I went to one of the in-stadium stores and bought a hat, and when I came back, my dad gave me crap about wasting my money on something so silly. I suppose he was right. But I still wear that hat when I go to games. And you know what else I still do? I still ask the person at the parking lot booth if the Mets are going to win. And I laugh because I know it's silly. Oh, and this goes without saying, but I never leave early, even if it rains.

     Going to a baseball game is something a lot of people do as a fun event. Maybe it's a family thing, or maybe just a couple of buddies catching a game after work. Or maybe it's two brothers keeping up a tradition by doing the thing that brought them so close as kids. It means something different to everyone. For my little brother and me, it means something special. People often ask me why I'm a Mets fan. Why I endure such endless suffering, when a few subway lines away sits a team almost always in first place and post-season-bound. Well, it's easy to root for a team that wins all the time. Being a true Mets fan is about loyalty and believing in your team no matter what. That's what my dad believed, and that's what he taught us (hear that, Alex and Matt?) It's about carrying that optimism into other aspects of your life and being appreciative of who and what you have. So you can keep the World Series parades and newspaper headlines. The Mets have given me decades of memories (certainly too many to list). They created a bond between my father and me that I will cherish forever. They've made my little brother and me the best of friends. They've inspired perfect tailgating festivities, with our close family friend manning the grill and imparting his love, wisdom, and guidance to two kids who needed it. Two kids, whose father (unbeknownst to them) asked this man to take them to games and keep an eye on them, a promise he keeps to this day and one my brother and I are extremely grateful for. Mets fans are hopeful. We're faithful to the end, and we always believe.

This was a particularly exciting time for Mets fans, not because we were going to win the pennant or dominate October, but because of one player on our team. I remember the day we signed him. Keep in mind that this was before social media took over the world, and before cell phones provided timely notifications. It was a time when you got your sports news by listening to the radio. My dad came up the stairs. It was morning, before school, and my little brother and I were on our way down the stairs. "Guess who we got?" he said. He had a wide smile that puffed his cheeks up. I wanted to take a guess, but I was afraid of being disappointed. He was so excited to tell us, and we couldn't believe the best hitter in baseball was now a New York Met.

  So there we were, sitting together in Shea, and hoping. That's what Mets fans do: we hope. The Mets had a lead going into the ninth inning, but the Phillies tied it in the top half. It came down to the bottom of the ninth. Anyone who argues that baseball lacks drama or intensity doesn't know his ass from a hole in the ground. This was drama, only intensified by my dad's dip in stamina. I knew he couldn't last much longer. It was a hot day, and he looked utterly exhausted. I know why he stayed though. It's the same reason any Mets fan stays to the end. Because that's what we do. We are a loyal bunch, we Mets fans. That, and my dad knew it meant a lot to us to stay to the end. There was always that chance, right? C'mon, you know the saying...YA GOTTA BELIEVE!

One out. Two more chances, otherwise extra innings. I just wanted the game to end so we could take my dad home. I remember sitting in my seat next to him, watching him out of the corner of my eye as he clung to whatever hope and energy he had left.

Then it happened. He stepped out of the on-deck circle, and walked toward the plate. His entrance music was blasting, and the crowd rose to its feet. Our favorite player up at bat in the ninth inning of a tied game with a chance to win it. I remember that moment so clearly. We were watching, hoping, and needing something special. And he gave it to us.

Our beloved catcher and my all-time favorite player, #31, Mike Piazza smashed a game-winning home run, and the crowd went wild. I looked at my dad, and he was smiling that same happy, cheek-puffing smile. The Mets won the game off the bat of our hero, and my dad was happy. And he deserved that, too.

I know I'll probably never have the chance to meet Mike Piazza. But I was at the game when the Mets retired his number. I went with my little brother. We stool there, side by side, wearing our Piazza jerseys. And when they removed the covering and revealed his 31 during the pre-game ceremony, we both smiled. We hugged each other, we cried a little, and we were happy, thinking how much our dad would have loved to be there.

My little brother and I have been best friends for as long as I can remember. Maybe it's because we were the youngest and had to stick together. Maybe it's because we had the least amount of time with our dad. Maybe it's because we're both Mets fans. Doesn't matter. He, like my dad of course, is a genuinely good person with a warm heart. We're all older now (that happens) and we have a gang of nephews who range in age. And while they love all their uncles, my little brother is their clear favorite, and for good reason. He truly loves children, and he's so naturally comfortable and good with them, a trait he undoubtedly got from our dad.

He'll make a wonderful father one day, and even though he's my little brother, I learn a lot from him about patience and practicality. He and I have been through some rough times together, but on that day when we stood together to celebrate a momentous occasion, we felt and shared true happiness.

Most Mets fans will remember Piazza's iconic blast after 9/11 when the Mets and all of New York needed something bright to lift our spirits. No doubt he gave that to us, and of course I'm grateful. But I would also suppose that any real fan has a favorite moment, a special memory that sticks out for some reason. That homerun on July 29 is mine. So no, I will probably never meet this man, but I know exactly what I'd say if I did. I'd tell him that he gave my dad a smile. That he hit the game-winning shot on the last Mets game I ever went to with my dad. And I'd say thank you.

Chapter 27

I remember standing in the funeral home wearing my oversized black suit, trying to take it all in, trying to acknowledge and somehow accept the reality of what was happening. There were family members all around me, many of whom I barely recognized. (Thanks, mother.) I remember walking outside every few minutes to catch my breath. It was hot out, but there were too many people inside. I needed to sort my thoughts; I needed to process it all, though I knew I couldn't. I understood that there would be time for grieving and all that after the fact, so I had just had to get through the next few draining hours.

I remember watching my sister talk to my aunts and uncles, people I hardly knew. She was so sad, yet so poised. She made her way from group to group, somehow keeping herself together. I remember being impressed by that. I walked around with my three brothers, giving and getting hugs, fighting back tears, chit chatting about the day's surreal quality. We'd break apart every few minutes or so to see friends and thank them for coming.

I remember seeing our family friend—the one who still takes my little brother and me to Mets games—and him hugging me. It meant a lot to me that he was there. He asked me how I was holding up, understanding that my "just fine" response was complete bullshit.

Seeing him did bring me some solace because I knew he understood what I was going through. I first met him when I was thirteen years old. He was my sister's boyfriend's (they got married years later) best friend. He owned a baseball card booth in our local mall, which, to a thirteen year-old boy who collected baseball cards, was the most amazing occupation conceivable. And he hired me. It was my first job. I worked for him on Saturdays for some cash, a few free packs of Fleer or Topps, the freedom of not being in my house for upwards of twelve hours (which was worth more than any amount of money), and some much-needed tough love. In many ways, he helped me grow up. Granted, I've always been immature for my age, but I was in dire need of some ass-kicking maturation. He taught me (I know this sounds ridiculous) how to eat without looking like a slob, how to conduct myself in a conversation with adults, how to man a cash register and count change without the register doing the math for me, how to answer a phone without sounding ignorant, and how to appreciate classic rock music instead of the lame crap I listened to. He taught me, in many ways, to be a man. He was like a big brother and a father figure rolled into one person, knowing that my own dad did his very best considering the circumstances. He also helped me to grow a backbone and stand up to my mother. I remember being thankful that an outsider corroborated how I felt about my mother, as he understood what went on in our home and how it affected my siblings and me. That day I stood up to my mother after she hit me with the salad dressing—I give myself the credit for having done it, but it was he who helped me build the confidence I needed behind it.

I worked for him for several years before the gas station, and he stuck with me through years of foolish behavior, through my dad's sickness and passing, and through many Mets losses. I can't put into words how thankful I am for everything that he has done for me and my little brother, for all the games he has taken us to and all the memories and life lessons he has given us. I knew he'd be there on that day, so I wasn't surprised to see him, but I was surely grateful.

I remember looking over into the corner of the large reception room. My boss (gas station) was there with his wife, and that meant a lot to me, too. He didn't have to be there. The guy, like our family friend and my dad, was a business owner and had plenty of work to do, but he was there. As a personal rule, therefore, I always try my hardest to at least make an appearance when someone I know loses someone. People remember who showed up and who didn't, and even if you don't say or do anything special, your presence speaks volumes.

Your absence does as well. I remember my boss was sitting on a large chair with his wife, and I when I walked over to him, he asked me a simple question that I wasn't prepared for. He asked me what I was going to do now. I gave him my honest answer: I had no idea.

    That was a thought that plagued me for a long time, because I really didn't know. My dad was gone. Nothing was changing that. I was a college dropout, and I didn't know if there was a point in changing that. My friends, some of whom drove hours from college to be by my side, would have to go back to school, and there wasn't a hell of a lot of motivation coming from anywhere. The hours of the funeral were frightening and understandingly uncomfortable, but at least I knew where I was supposed to be.

    What *could* I do? What was I *supposed* to do? Go back to school? What for? Work more hours? Find a second job? And a new problem emerged: I had to find a new place to live. Shortly after dad died, mother decided she had had enough, so she packed her belongings, sold our house and my dad's business for who-the-hell-knows-what, and bought herself a new white Mercedes Benz and a condo in Florida. Bye, mother. And bye, house, too.

  Believe me, no tears were shed upon her departure, but saying goodbye to our house hurt. I'm not an overly sentimental person, and it's not like my house was the birthplace of a storybook childhood, but it bothered me nonetheless. Perhaps it was the way it was so haphazardly discarded. My dad worked hard for that house, he worked every day of his life to keep it up and running and to keep us sheltered and provided for. She just let it go without thinking twice.

  I drove by the house a few months ago. Some builder purchased it from my mother and did an impressive flip job, making it even more HGTV-worthy. I parked outside for a few minutes and watched it. There was an unfamiliar car in the newly configured and freshly paved driveway, and I couldn't help but imagine the new family who inhabited it. No jealousy, no bitterness; honestly, I just wonder about what it's like in there so many years later. I looked at my old bedroom window and thought about who could be living there now. Maybe there's a new little boy living in my old room, making memories with his siblings and wondering where life is going to take him.

It took me a few years to do it, but I called my mother one day. I knew my brothers had spoken to her on occasion, and perhaps I felt compelled to out of guilt. I'm not sure. Believe it or not, I even went down to visit a couple times. I don't know, I guess it was the right thing to do. But every time I spoke to her, every time I saw her, I hated myself. I hated who I became. I turned into this short-tempered, defensive introvert. I was so tense and irritable. It was as though all of my worst qualities came to the surface and took me over. I was completely uncomfortable, saw no purpose in the visit itself other than trying to do "the right thing," and looked forward to either hanging up the phone or getting back on the plane (even though I hate planes). I decided I couldn't do it anymore. No more phone calls. No more visits. No more communication.

The last time I spoke to mother, well, I can't even tell you. It's been years. Many years. And honestly, it's better that way. There will never be any kind of mother-son relationship. There will never be any restitution, or common ground, or mutual understanding. We are different people, and I'm a better person when she is not in my life. I know it's hard for someone to contemplate that—a son who doesn't speak to his mother. But it's a decision I had to make.

Do I feel guilty about that? I know it sounds horrible that a son wouldn't visit his own mother. That a son wouldn't even pick up a phone to speak to her, to ask her how she is. No Happy Birthday phone calls or Mother's Day cards. I don't claim to be a perfect person. Maybe I don't have the strength to forgive and forget. Maybe I've just written her off and put her out of my mind and out of my life. Maybe one day I'll feel differently, and yes, maybe that one day will be too late. But the truth is, I don't feel guilty. I believe that as a man, I have control over my own life and who I allow to be a part of it. Yeah, this is me believing what I believe and standing my ground. It's a choice I get to make. I've made it. She doesn't make the cut.

But there was still the problem of being homeless.

Chapter 28

My sister had recently bought a house close to where we grew up, and thankfully she had an extra two bedrooms. Even more thankfully, she and her husband invited my little brother and me into their home, knowing we had nowhere else to go. We were homeless. Once mother rid herself of our house, the Incorporated Village of Belle Terre became a memory. My sister and brother-in-law were married, had an infant, discussed the possibility of having another child, and had their hands full with a new house and a young family, but they let us stay with them. They didn't have to do that. For that, and for them, I will forever be grateful.

Likewise, I will always be grateful for my brother-in-law's mother. I know that sounds like a stretch, like someone I wouldn't necessarily be close to, but I'll tell ya', that woman is a saint if I've ever seen one. Her house was quite close to theirs, and I spent a lot of time there. She knew how close I was to my father, she understood the kind of unavoidable relationship I had with my mother, and she knew that sometimes, all it took was a home-cooked meal and a hug to make me feel better. Sorry if that sounds childish, but it's the truth. I don't care how old you are—those two gifts are priceless. She made her home warm and welcoming, she embraced my brothers and me with open arms, and she did her very best to fill a gaping void in our lives. I remember sitting at her kitchen table after my dad died. The food was on the stove, still warm, and there was a pot of coffee freshly made. I remember her sitting next to me. She didn't say much, but she listened. And when I openly cried, I felt no shame, no embarrassment. I'm not much of a crier, and God knows I tried as hard as I could to keep it in. But she let me cry, and she hugged me, and she loved me. And for that, I will forever be thankful.

So there I was, living in a bedroom in my sister's house (that sounds quite pathetic when I say it aloud), sharing a bathroom with a toddler (which had its fair share of entertainment, I'll admit), enjoying an occasional meal at the warm house down the road, and doing my best to get back on some kind of track. It wasn't long before a routine had established itself yet again, and my full-time hours at the gas station became my rock. It sounds bizarre, I know, but I felt comfortable there. I sincerely appreciated what my sister and brother-in-law were doing for me and my little brother, but I felt guilty, as if I was invading their life together. I could sense their frustration with me as time went on, and our relationship suffered because of it. Don't get me wrong, there was still plenty of love in all directions, but I knew I had to leave before my welcome was worn out.

In all honesty, my sister married an awesome guy. For one, he treats my sister the way anyone would want his sister treated. For another, my dad loved him, and that speaks volumes to me. But besides all that, he's a genuinely good person with an impeccable moral compass. He sees being a husband and a father and a care-giver as his most important responsibilities, and nothing comes before any of that. And something else I love about him—he's very affectionate. I don't know if I've ever shaken his hand in all the years I've known him. With my brother-in-law, you're getting a big bear hug every time you see him, and I have no objection whatsoever. There's a lot to be learned from a guy like that, and I've looked up to him since the first day he came to our house. And now, here I was, living in his house because he knew I was out of options and because he loved me. He and I have always bonded over several things, and I was watching our relationship take a hit. I owed it to him, to my sister, and to my dad to do something. Living there was a wonderful blessing, but it couldn't be permanent.

I increased my hours at the gas station considerably. It gave me some purpose. It was a familiar place, and that brought me ease and solace. I did re-enroll in college, not with a definitive objective necessarily, but to at least move in some kind of seemingly positive direction. It made me feel less guilty about living in their house, too—I wasn't hanging out at bars or doing drugs or gambling or being a criminal. When I wasn't home, I was either working or in class. That's something, right?

I went back to finish what I started at SCC, which included filling my day with electives to satisfy requirements. I was never much for reading, and although I earned decent essay grades in high school (God knows it wasn't because of my hard work or diligence), I hated English. I detested most of my English teachers growing up because they were boring, lifeless drones who were as old as they were crotchety, and being in their classes was torture.

I had to take an English elective.

The ones about this era of literature or that realm of garbage or this famous writer did not strike my fancy. No interest, no, thank you. Wasn't my thing. I scrolled through the list and found something that seemed slightly stimulating, not completely torturous. It was a class on creative writing. So, I signed up and went in with an honestly open mind and zero expectations.

As I said before, I'm not one for clichés, and I certainly won't bullshit you. But there was something about the way the professor taught, something about his approach to the craft of writing that got me. It intrigued me. He intrigued me. For the first time in my academic life, I found myself putting forth a real effort. I didn't even know what was happening to me, but I started to care about what I was writing, the assignments I turned in, what I brought to and from his class. I valued his opinion and appreciated his constructive criticism. I doubt he even knew my name, but his opinion meant something to me, and I tried to impress him with my writing. Suddenly I found this interest, this skill that was dormant for so long, buried under pounds of laziness. Yeah, this guy had a way about him. I remember he was funny as hell, too. Didn't dress like an English professor, either. He wore jeans, t-shirts, had long hair, cursed, told funny stories, was occasionally inappropriate (not in a weird, creepy, Dateline sort of way), spoke fluent sarcasm, and called people out when they deserved it, unlike the high school teachers who doled out meaningless grades and empty praises to the privileged children of entitled parents. Something clicked, all right.

By the time the semester ended, I had something I had never experienced before, and it felt good. I had a definitive direction. I had a clear goal. I didn't know if it was realistic or foolish, but it was a goal, and I was going to go for it.

I was going to be an English teacher.

Chapter 29

School became something different, something it had never been. And it surprised me. I actually cared. Having a goal motivated me to give a crap. And I'm proud to say I finished Suffolk (okay, it took me a little longer than two years, but I still did it) with a respectable GPA and was on my way to continue my college education at St. Joseph's College in Patchogue: Long Island's teacher factory.

I used the summer months between semesters to crank up hours at the station. And my position changed, too. I had taken a keen interest in cars—following my brother's footsteps, I suppose—and spent my downtime in the shop with the technicians who had become like a family to me. Well, actually, that sounded too flowery, and I promised to be honest with you. What actually happened was I ditched the full-serve pumps and hung out in the shop all day with the mechanics because they were cool and funny and taught me things about cars and sometimes my boss (understandably) got pissed because the full-serve customers started honking. There, that's better.

    And how about this? One of the mechanics, who specialized in basic maintenance work, left for another job. That opened a position and upset my boss because now he'd have to go through the interview and hiring process, hoping a new guy would work out. Thankfully, he accepted my proposition and let me try. No harm, right? If I failed, I could be "fired" and I could go back to ignoring the incessant, lazy full-serve customers. If I did well, I'd get a mechanic shirt with my name on it and save my boss a hassle. Win-win. Now, I understand that changing oil and fixing flat tires and replacing light bulbs and wiper blades didn't make me a grade-A automotive technician with a future at BMW, and I know it probably doesn't make much sense, but I felt truly proud of myself for doing it. I got to call myself a mechanic, and that was neat.

    I stayed focused, asked the other (actual) technicians a ton of annoying questions, and ultimately learned a skill. I learned how to do something that not everyone can do. I worked hard every day, I sweat my ass off in the summer and froze it off in the winter, I got my hands dirty, and I finally learned what it meant to work for a living. It felt good. Really good. I set a goal, albeit a reasonable one, I worked toward it, and I achieved it. I paid my own rent (granted, my sister and brother-in-law charged me only minimal rent to cover groceries), I paid for my own car and the insurance and gas to go with it, and for the first time in my life, I felt like I was on my way to making my dad proud. Even if he wasn't around to see it.

Not that I'm aiming to evoke another *awwww*, but I also had established a long-term relationship with a girl I met while working at the station. Nothing says "I love you" like an oil change, right? Again, I found myself with a beautiful girl, and again, I found myself in love. I fell pretty hard for this one, and as I progressed through school and observing classrooms and student teaching and shaving time off my oil changes and state inspections, I felt confident that I had found the future missus.

I was in a good place, finally standing on solid ground, as if I, at last, got my shit together. I was working out hard, putting in a ton of hours, making money, doing well in my classes, and I felt pride for having a long-term girlfriend. She and I dated for over three years, and although it wasn't perfect, and although I admittedly had no idea how to actually be someone's boyfriend (I'm a slow learner sometimes), and although we had plenty of glaring differences between us, I loved her. That's the truth. I could blame immaturity, I suppose. Or I could blame my parents for not showing me a proper model of how to treat a loved one. But those are just excuses, and you know how I feel about those.

Occasionally, when you fix someone's flat tire or squeeze in a quick, walk-in oil change, you get a tip. It didn't happen often, but when it did, it was greatly appreciated as it went directly into "the fund." I was working full-time, around sixty weekly hours during the summer and forty during the semester, but I was also trying to pay my way through school to minimize the loans I'm still repaying. And I was never a good saver. But I was able to put away something each week. The tips helped. My girlfriend came from a wealthy family. They were used to money, and so was she. And it was understandably important to her. Not that I felt inferior, because I honestly didn't, but I did feel like I had something to prove. The fund didn't grow quickly, but in time, it would get me into a jewelry store. Yes, I had another goal. I wasn't aiming for Tiffany's, and I knew anything I bought wouldn't weigh her hand down, but I wanted something special to show her how much she meant to me, even if it wasn't the most expensive thing in the store.

  It's nobody's fault. I wasn't able to admit that at the time, but I saw it years later. I was consumed by school and work, so was she, and we were headed in different directions. Our differences became more apparent and more difficult to ignore. I suppose I saw it, but I wasn't going to admit it, and I certainly wasn't going to do anything about it. Evidently, she didn't share my restraint. After having dinner together one night after work, she said "we need to talk." No good conversation ever starts with that.

Part VI: 8...9...

Chapter 30

People break up all the time. People fall out of love. It happens. But it hit me hard. And it took me a long time to get over her. This isn't easy to admit, but I fell into a depression. I had experienced (understandably, I assume) symptoms after my dad passed, but I was getting better. When she ended our relationship, the depression came back with a vengeance.

As a disclaimer, let me clarify that I don't use the word "depression" as an expression, as in I felt like shit because my girlfriend dumped me. I would never insult anyone who suffers from depression by using it as a euphemistic punchline. I mean I was depressed. With entry-level courses behind me, I found myself in demanding classrooms with no-nonsense professors who were anything but lenient or forgiving. My writing used to blow professors' hair back at SCC, but the nuns who ran SJC saw through fluff. They were a tough audience, and I was struggling. I was physically exhausted from working so many hours in the shop. My relationship with my sister and brother-in-law was becoming increasingly volatile because, quite frankly, I was invading their home and not pulling my weight. My motivation was rapidly depleting as was my confidence and energy. I thought I had my act together. I thought I had everything figured out. I didn't. I was slipping, questioning my own ambitions, my own abilities, my own future.

I, once again, thought of giving up. I felt like I was spinning on a wheel for no reason. I was faking a smile to get through the day, and I found little reason to get up every morning, knowing I wouldn't accomplish much besides getting through the day. I started to slack in the gym, I shut out friends and family, and I let myself stay down. I avoided social gatherings, ignored my phone when it rang, and felt like each day was a chore. I stayed in my room as much as I could, mistreated those around me because I couldn't get out of my own way, and I didn't see any light at the end of a long, dreary tunnel.

If you're wondering if I ever thought about taking my own life, the answer (honesty, as promised) is yes. I thought about it. I thought about the method and the note and the location. I wondered who, if anyone, would be upset about it. Of course, my family would be shocked and sad and all that, but I figured they'd move on eventually. I saw it as a viable option. It's a bad sign when you start rationalizing that sort of thing.

I remember my (now ex) girlfriend had an aunt who we used to see on holidays. She was a teacher nearing retirement and the parent of boys who were, in her mind, destined for success, and she was kind enough to habitually remind me of how tough the teaching market was and how slim the odds of landing a job would be, especially in a field like English. All the local colleges, as was so aptly explained, spill a batch of wanna-be, dime-a-dozen English teachers into the applicant pool at the end of each semester, so making yourself stand out was, at best, a long shot. I know she didn't say what she said to be hurtful. I actually think she was trying to help me. But it bothered me, what she said, and I remember thinking about her words even months later. It's amazing how much of an impact someone's words can be, positive or negative. That's something I always try to keep in mind. Anyway, I was single and hopeless, questioning my once-certain goal. The direction I was so sure-footedly going down was losing both clarity and appeal.

Being a mechanic was fun, but I knew it wouldn't make me a living. It could for others, but not for me. I wasn't good enough to ever be a real top-end technician, and even though my boss made me feel appreciated and gave consistent raises and incentive pay for extra ass-busting work, my pay—or any pay for someone with my skill level—would never support a mortgage or a family or a fruitful future. So I questioned that, too.

I didn't want to face it. Certainly didn't want to admit it. But I couldn't help but feel that I was letting my dad down again. That's what hurt the worst. Slipping in school, devastated in love, spinning my wheels but trying desperately to hang on. And it hurt. And depression doesn't just go away when the sun comes up. You can't just will it or wish it away. You can't just decide to turn it off. To this day, I still experience symptoms of it at times. But at that point in my life, I truly felt knocked down, maybe even out. Was ending my life the answer? Was that really what this was coming to? I didn't know what else to do. I didn't know what I was supposed to do. I felt alone. I felt lost. I was in pain, and I was scared.

Close your eyes.

Take a deep breath.

And then another deep breath.

Focus on one thing, not several.

Stay focused and don't give up.

Don't ever give up on yourself.

You can do this.

You are not alone. You have people who love you, family who supports you, and there is still something left in your heart.

Get up.

Part VII: Keep Moving Forward

Chapter 31

When you get to the climactic fight of a Rocky flick, you find yourself consumed by frustration, clinging to hope (kind of like watching a Mets game). Rocky can barely stand. He has taken a savage beating, and even though you know how it's going to turn out, you're worried that the next punch will knock him down for good. How could he possibly take any more?

We all get knocked down though, right? We've all felt that at some point—that feeling of hopelessness. That feeling of having taken too much. Life has this ability to give amazing ass-kickings, to knock us down. Some of us stay down for a long time. Some of us, forever. And some of us choose to stay down because, frankly speaking, it's easier. It's easier to look in that mirror and feel sorry for yourself. It's easier to look at others with envy, assuming their lives are infinitely better than yours. It's easier to blame someone for where or who you are. But what's the point of that? When you look back at your life years or decades later, what can you feel besides regret? At that point, you've become a master of excuses, having accomplished nothing and having nobody to blame besides yourself.

    The fact of the matter is that we all have control of our lives to a degree. We all have that choice. Maybe not when we're kids or going through school, and we can't control who our parents are or what kind of house or home we live in, but eventually we get to decide who and what and where we want to be. We get to make choices. We get to pick our goals, and we can work as hard as we want to reach them, or we can choose to give up on them when the path becomes a merciless gauntlet. We can't always choose when and how we get knocked down, but we can decide what to do once we're there. It's not easy to pick yourself up and keep fighting, I know that. It's not easy to, in the face of depression, get your ass up in the morning and focus on a goal and put forth an earnest effort to reach it. It's not easy. There's no trick, no gimmick. No magic pill, no simple solution. It takes self-confidence, even though you've run out. It takes patience, even though that's depleted. It takes courage and fortitude and resilience and perseverance. It takes heart.

    I was down. Knocked right on my ass on more than one occasion. And there were times when I didn't know if I could get up. And if I could get up, I wouldn't know what to do when I got there. Maybe I was even afraid of what would happen when I did get on my feet. But that's no excuse to stay down. Staying down is a choice, and not one I was going to make. Yes, I was depressed. Yes, I thought of killing myself. And although I never sought counseling, I did lean on those close to me. I had to. That's not a sign of weakness; it doesn't indicate a lack of strength. It's realizing that sometimes you need help or guidance or love or support or a combination of all of the above. That's what my family means to me. That's what my brothers and sister mean to me.

Remember that, Alex and Matt. Always remember that.

I don't know where I'd be without my siblings. Each of them is special for individual reasons, and each one, in his/her own way, makes me feel like dad is still here in some ways. Keeping his memory and his dying wish alive is important to all of us. And I'm proud to say we've done a pretty good job at honoring it (thanks, sis). We're all close. We depend on each other, we support each other, and we unconditionally love each other. That's what a family does. That what a family is. Most of us live close, and so we spend weekends and holidays together. We celebrate birthdays and have barbeques, we've done weddings and Bar Mitzvahs, and we've done funerals. We've done it all together. Some of us have become parents, holding dad in our hearts as we raise our children with love and laughter. Dad has been gone for a long time, and we've all moved on in our own ways, but every time we get together, every time we watch one of the kids blow out a birthday candle that sits atop a Carvel cake, every time my sister (re)tells a funny story or one of my brothers says something funny to make our cheeks puff up with smiles, every time my little brother and I watch the Mets take the field, every time we gather around someone's kitchen table for pizza bagels (dad was an exquisite chef and pizza bagels were one of his specialties), every time we hug one of our many nephews whose names all carry on his legacy, we hold dad in our hearts. So even though he's gone, he's still here, in all of us.

  I have an amazing family, and I realize that despite an *interesting* childhood, I am quite blessed to have these wonderful people in my life. That's what I *choose* to focus on.

  And so, I knew I was down. I knew I had almost nothing left. I knew it all could have ended at any moment. But I also knew that I was worth more than that. I realized that if I was this blessed to have such a wonderful family, such amazing siblings and people around me who care, I could find a way. And if my dad was in some better place looking down on me, I owed it to him to try. I couldn't give up. Couldn't throw in the towel.

He deserves more than that. And you know what? So do I.

If Mickey was in my corner, he'd tell me to get up and fight. He'd say, "Get up, you bum!" That's what I'd tell Alex and Matt to do (maybe not in those words). I'd tell them the importance of believing in yourself, of taking the hits and the falls, but never giving up. Making yourself get up. And like when a pitcher brushes you back with a high fast one and you hit the dirt, you don't give him the satisfaction of dusting yourself off. Fuck that. You stand up, you get back in the box, and you make him pay with the next one. You don't feel sorry for yourself. And you don't give up on your goals and your dreams. You are better than that.

So you know what I did? I took Mickey's advice. I held my father in my heart, I leaned on those around me for support, I drew a few deep breaths, and I followed my own advice.

    I got up.

Chapter 32

Hi. My name is Lee Markowitz, and this is my story.

I'm in my mid-thirties now. Okay, more like late thirties, but who's keeping track? It's the holiday season, and I just finished putting the lights on the outside of the house. I grew up in a Jewish family, so I'm new at this house-decorating thing, but I'm getting the hang of it. And I love it.

Samantha, my beautiful, encouraging wife of almost five years, is sitting at our dining room table wrapping presents while our two-year-old son Alexander helps her by putting the finished ones (that aren't for him, of course) under the tree. I come in from the cold, and I catch myself standing there watching them; and I pause for a moment to take it in and breathe a sigh of true happiness and content. We all need to do that every once in a while—just pause for a moment and take it all in. Take inventory of our lives. Recognize the blessings we have, the people who matter the most. Just like taking a good look at yourself in the mirror, we all need to do it occasionally. It keeps us in check. And these days, it's not a chore I dread. I can look in the mirror, right into the eyes of the man looking back at me, and feel genuinely proud of myself, not because of what I've accomplished necessarily, but because I never gave up on myself.

This is my family, and this is our home.

Alex uses the break between present placing to eat his dry cheerios out of his plastic bowl and sip his milk that he occasionally spills (and that's just fine with me) and play with the countless Thomas the Tank Engine toys that litter our floor. (They're lots of fun, especially when you step on one while barefoot.) Samantha keeps her bottle of water next to her tea mug and gives me a smile when she sees me. Her belly has only slightly started to show, although she insists she's a blob. There's a plate of half-eaten Girl Scout cookies, but I refrain from making a joke about Mommy being the cookie monster. (Alex and I will giggle about that later.) Matthew is due in early May, and his room still needs plenty of work, but I'll get to it. I've learned a lot from my older brothers about house repairs and painting and all that, so it's a project I feel comfortable tackling. And I know my brothers will happily pop by to lend a helping hand and to play with their nephew. It's a Sunday afternoon, and we both have work tomorrow, but the Sunday night blues don't seem to come around this time of year.

After we put Alex to sleep around seven, we'll sit in our living room by the fire, and Sam will make me watch one of those horribly predicable and cheesy Hallmark Christmas movies. She loves them. She cries during the sad scenes. (She'll blame the pregnancy hormones.) She cries because someone's mother passes away or has already passed away, and that reminds her of her own mom. She can't help it, and I get it. Even though time makes it easier, as they say, the pain remains with us. And on that note, I have to say, not too many guys luck out in the mother-in-law department, but I did. Sam's mom was an amazing woman—strong, smart, and loving. I'm lucky because Sam is just like her, and I know that would make her mom proud. It's tough for her, raising a family and being a wife and not having the support her mother provided her whole life. But that doesn't stop her. Sure, she misses her, and of course she has her moments of weakness, as do we all, but she's a strong woman. She's an amazing wife, nurturing, and caring, and I couldn't imagine my life without her. I knew it when I met her, that I had found someone truly special. Someone who is understanding and loyal and kind and genuine. And I couldn't ask for a better mommy for our two boys.

  I lucked out in the father-in-law department, too. I loved my dad very much, and I miss him a lot. And it hurts that my sons will never know him and that my wife never met him. He would have absolutely loved her. He would have adored all of his grandsons, too. Sometimes while I'm watching Alex sit on the den carpet and play with his toys and puzzles, I picture my dad here, sitting and playing with him. I'm not a religious person, and I would never preach anything of the sort, but I like to believe that my dad is somewhere watching over his kids and his grandkids. But you know what? I've never seen two happier people than when Sam's father is with his grandson. I think it's good for both of them. I love watching them together, how much it means to each of them. How much love they have for each other. How much they mean to each other. And I like to think that Sam's mom looks down from time-to-time (hopefully not all the time) and smiles for the same reasons.

So I'll sit next to Sam on our cozy hand-me-down couch, I'll give her a tissue, and I'll hold her hand as we await some more lame romance scenes with too much fake snow in a town with too many Christmas decorations. And I can't help but smile. I make fun of these movies a lot, and it drives Sam nuts, but also entertains her—I catch her smirking or giggling sometimes at my incessantly obnoxious commentary. I can't really judge her though, considering I won't pass up an opportunity to catch a Stallone flick. We all have our vices.

Some of these holiday movies start with a tragedy, like a parent dying or a kid growing up in a home that isn't loving or nurturing. But you know what? There's always a happy ending. And who doesn't love a happy ending, right? The holiday season provides the needed magic, the music draws you in, the guy gets the girl, and everything has a way of working out. Maybe that's why I secretly like them, too. (*Shhh*, don't tell Sam.)

And here's some irony that would surely make my dad laugh: my wife, whom I love more than words can say, is wearing her Yankee pajama pants. That's right, I married a devout Yankee fan. She takes after her dad. Wouldn't you know it? I'm not sure how that's going to play out with Alex and Matt, but we'll find a way to get through it. Talk about sending your kids to therapy, right?

Anyway, the holiday season—as much as we look forward to and cherish it—will come to an end before we know it, and we'll both head back to work. That's where we met: at work. I know, cheesy, huh? Two teachers fall in love and live happily ever after.

I'll say it for you: *Awwwwwwwwwww*.

I suppose there aren't too many people who look forward to going to work, but the truth is that I don't mind it. I love my job, I'm thankful for the life it affords my family and me, and (tooting my own horn here) I'm pretty darn good at it. I worked hard to get it, and now that I have it, I work even harder. And I think that would make my dad proud.

When the holiday break is over, I'll wake up nice and early. I'll hit the gym, I'll shower and shave, and then I'll get dressed and go to work. I'll walk into my eleventh-grade English classroom. I'll look at the pictures of my family tacked up on the board next to my desk, and I'll smile at the giant Rocky poster on the wall behind. I'll sit at my desk and take a grateful breath as I wait for my students to walk in, and just before they do, I'll look at the small framed picture of my dad that sits right next to my computer. It sounds silly, I know, but this way he can watch me work.

www.ingramcontent.com/pod-product-compliance
Lightning Source LLC
Chambersburg PA
CBHW031443040426
42444CB00007B/940